Smokies Chronicle

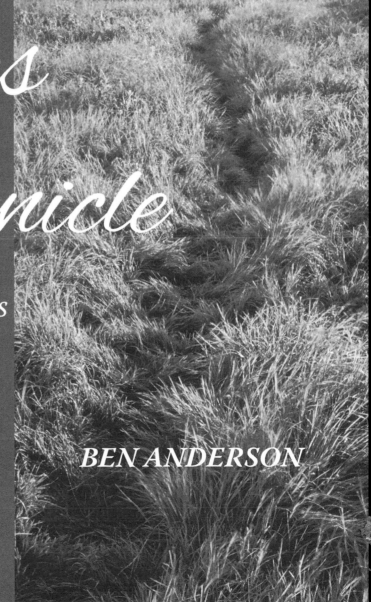

Smokies

Chronicle

A Year of Hiking in Great Smoky Mountains National Park

BEN ANDERSON

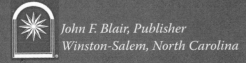

John F. Blair, Publisher
Winston-Salem, North Carolina

JOHN F. BLAIR, PUBLISHER

1406 Plaza Drive
Winston-Salem, North Carolina 27103
blairpub.com

Library of Congress Cataloging-in-Publication Data

Names: Anderson, Ben, 1951- author.
Title: Smokies chronicle : a year of hiking in Great Smoky Mountains National
    Park / Ben Anderson.
Description: Winston-Salem, North Carolina : John F. Blair, Publisher, [2017]
    | Includes index.
Identifiers: LCCN 2017010669 (print) | LCCN 2017012946 (ebook) | ISBN
    9780895876942 (e-book) | ISBN 9780895876935 (pbk. : alk. paper)
Subjects: LCSH: Hiking--Great Smoky Mountains National Park (N.C. and
    Tenn.)--Guidebooks. | Trails--Great Smoky Mountains National Park (N.C.
    and Tenn.)--Guidebooks. | Great Smoky Mountains National Park (N.C. and
    Tenn.)--Guidebooks.
Classification: LCC GV199.42.G73 (ebook) | LCC GV199.42.G73 A52 2017 (print)
    | DDC 796.5109768/89--dc23
LC record available at https://lccn.loc.gov/2017010669

10 9 8 7 6 5 4 3 2 1

Cover Photo: "Early Morning View on Gregory Bald," courtesy of Kevin Adams; kadamsphoto.com
Cover Design: Anna B. Sutton
Interior Design: Debra Hampton
Layout: The Roberts Group

For Ben and Rob,
who've given us
our best times in the woods

Table of Contents

Preface

With any number of ceremonies and programs planned across the country to celebrate the National Park Service Centennial in 2016, I decided to mark the milestone in a personal way of my own design: by venturing into the vastness of the Great Smoky Mountains as frequently as possible throughout the year. I aimed for three to four day hikes each month, spaced evenly as practicable over the year, with a target of ten outings during each season. In doing so, I revisited some trails and places I was familiar with from previous hiking and backpacking excursions, often through my role as a backcountry volunteer for more than twenty years. But these journeys were different, even on trails I had hiked before, as I had the goal of seeking deeper insights into the park through its extensive network of established trails. Although I hiked sections of the Appalachian Trail here and there, my focus was on the hundreds of miles of official trails elsewhere in the 520,000-acre park. I should add that partly because I intended to hike alone on most outings—typically discouraged by the park service—I planned to do very little off-trail hiking. The maintained trails would provide more than enough adventures, particularly in less than ideal weather. Those experiences, encompassing part or all of nearly half the park's trails, were chronicled by handwritten observations, noted in a treasured, thirty-year-old *Hiking Notes* book. I later took the notes and wrote narratives about each hike for the pages that follow. As with watching a baseball game, it may not be necessary to keep a backcountry scorecard of sorts in order to enjoy the woods, but doing so really does seem to make the experience more meaningful.

On heavily and lightly traveled trails alike, my focus for the year was day hiking spanning the seasons, in reasonably good weather, often on routes that required using more than one trail. Day hiking, of course, doesn't demand the extensive preparation required for backpacking. With the latter, cooking, bedding, and shelter join adequate food, water, clothing, and footwear as vital concerns. But day hiking in rugged areas such as the Great Smoky Mountains should never be dismissed as a risk-free activity, especially on the more demanding trails in potentially rough weather. Although most paths in the park are well maintained and marked with accurate mileages, it is easy to underestimate the difficulty of steep, rocky trails and hazardous stream crossings, especially after heavy rainfall. The potential for injury or wandering off on a wrong course is always present, especially for hikers unaccustomed to the often-challenging terrain and footing. Rapid changes in weather can occur as well. Thus, despite the good fortune of not previously facing a major crisis on the trail, I did need to remain aware of the fact that any number of mishaps can and do occur in the woods, especially without proper planning. Hiking alone also requires greater caution than hiking with a group, including notifying at least one other person of the planned travel route and estimated time in the woods. But with these issues in mind, and with no plans to hike in severe conditions, I began 2016 with little reservation about mostly solo hiking throughout the year.

Even during milder mountain winters—and a few in recent years actually have been unusually harsh—high-elevation trails in the Smokies are often inaccessible. Fully aware of possible severe weather especially up high, I planned to hike in the lower elevations early and late in the year. Fortunately, there is quite a bit of hiking in the park below three thousand feet in elevation, where heavy snowfall is uncommon. The Smokies' higher terrain could wait until late winter or early spring, and, in fact, would be welcome territory once the summer heat and humidity of the lowlands started to build. Still, I needed to carefully choose my routes, especially during the colder months. Although some hikers and backpackers may relish the challenge, I confess to having little interest in being caught in a snow or ice storm while deep in the backcountry. I also had no desire to punish myself on forced marches, even if I did plan to embark on quite a few lengthy and strenuous hikes. As nineteenth-century outdoorsman George Washington Sears (a.k.a. Nessmuk) observed, we often get it rough enough *away* from the woods.

After living for thirty years within striking distance of dozens of Smokies trails on the North Carolina side of the park, I began 2016 not having hiked many Tennessee trails. Yes, I had hiked some of the more compelling paths on the Tennessee side such as The Boulevard, Chimney Tops, and Alum Cave—trails that seemed too inviting not to hike, despite the longer drive time. But primarily because the trailheads were not as accessible for me, I was largely unfamiliar with Smokies trails in Tennessee at the beginning of the year. Then again, there were a number of trails on the North Carolina side that I either hadn't hiked in many years or had not hiked at all. I hoped to chip away at those deficiencies throughout the year as I furthered my goal of a fresh look at the park. I looked forward to revisiting spectacular places such as Shuckstack (also among my favorite Smokies place names), and to discovering stunning sites in Tennessee, such as Albright Grove and Ramsey Cascades.

As the year progressed and the miles began to pile up, I set a goal of hiking four hundred miles on all or part of at least sixty different trails. In surpassing that goal by year's end, I walked more than one million steps, as it takes about twenty-five hundred steps to cover one mile. For the year, the mileage was roughly equivalent to the distance from my home in Asheville to the Georgia/Florida line on Interstate 95. Although I hiked all the miles on day outings rather than backpacking trips, a total of four nights of frontcountry camping in spring and fall facilitated completion of a handful of hikes by reducing driving time. I also shifted from light hiking shoes at the start of the year to sturdier boots, as the hikes predictably lengthened with warmer weather and more daylight. Along the way, I enjoyed many pleasant brief conversations with fellow hikers I encountered, including two memorable exchanges with a fit and friendly young couple from the Netherlands near the end of the year. Conversely, I did not see a mortal soul on several moderately long hikes—the solitude was undisturbed as I hiked deep into the woods.

My year of hiking took me to many parts of the second largest national park in the East. Without exception, each area was engaging in its own way. I hope this account of my travels across much of the Great Smoky Mountains fully reflects that.

Acknowledgments

Successful completion of this project could not have been accomplished without the expertise and guidance of the staff of John F. Blair, Publisher. I am fortunate to join the ranks of writers Blair has published since its inception in the mid-1950s. Special thanks go to my editor, Carolyn Sakowski, for her keen editorial eye. My wife, Karen Anderson, also provided vital assistance with her suggestions regarding the manuscript.

Although many fine books have been written about the Great Smoky Mountains, I can trace the primary inspiration for writing my own Smokies book to three people who made Bryson City, North Carolina, their home in the twentieth century: Horace Kephart and, decades later, George and Elizabeth Ellison. In my view their written and artistic work on the Smokies and environs is unsurpassed, if not without lasting controversy in the case of Kephart's seminal book, *Our Southern Highlanders*. A number of illuminating works dealing specifically with the Smokies park also have blazed a path for me.

Indirectly but undoubtedly, I owe a substantial debt—as does anyone who has spent even a few hours in the Smokies—to the people who helped make the park happen more than eighty years ago, despite daunting obstacles. Early park advocates Anne and Willis Davis of Knoxville, Tennessee; National Park Service Director (1929-1933) Horace Albright; philanthropist John D. Rockefeller Jr.—these individuals and many others were instrumental in the creation of the park that hundreds of millions have enjoyed since 1934. The same can be said of President Franklin D. Roosevelt, who not only made a significant federal allotment that was needed to complete funding for park land acquisitions, but also created the Civilian Conservation Corps, which built numerous facilities and trails during the park's early years. Without these forward-thinking people, there would be no park for visitors like me to enjoy. And the park, if not flawless, would not be the gem it is to visit today but for the efforts of countless dedicated employees and volunteers over the years. I also am personally grateful for the assistance many of those employees have generously given me in various ways.

Introduction

Although Yellowstone National Park became the world's first national park in 1872, the National Park Service itself wasn't established until 1916. On August 25 of that year, President Woodrow Wilson signed the Organic Act to belatedly create a bureau of the federal government charged with managing the relatively small number of national parks existing at that time. Before 1916, management fell to various government agencies and departments, including the War Department. Thus, 2016—not 1972—was regarded and celebrated as the centennial of our national parks. By its centennial, the National Park Service had grown to comprise more than four hundred national park units, including fifty-nine designated as national parks, with the vast majority of the latter located west of the Mississippi River.

In 1916, the idea of a national park in the Great Smoky Mountains had not progressed beyond a determined but unsuccessful southern Appalachian park movement led by Dr. Chase P. Ambler of Asheville, North Carolina. That movement flamed out about 1905. In fact, there were no national parks in the eastern United States until Lafayette National Park (now known as Acadia) was established in Maine in 1919. The half-million acres in Tennessee and North Carolina that eventually formed the Smokies park were dotted by several thousand homesteads and separate tracts in 1916, even as much of the rugged mountain forestland was being furiously logged by large timber companies that dramatically altered much of the landscape. The Smokies' great forests were being leveled cut by cut—ravaged rather than managed.

But the concept of a park in the Great Smoky Mountains gained significant momentum in the mid-1920s, due to heavy promotion by influential and persuasive residents of both states, including *Our Southern Highlanders* author Horace Kephart. By 1934, with the vital help of a $5 million matching gift from John D. Rockefeller Jr. and an unprecedented park acquisition allotment of $1.5 million by President Franklin D. Roosevelt, Great Smoky Mountains National Park became a reality. And certainly not at the expense of any other area, as the Smokies' scenery, significance, and biological diversity was and is unparalleled in the southern Appalachians. Upon its creation, the park became by far the largest national park east of the Mississippi, a distinction later assumed by Everglades National Park upon its establishment after World War II. President Roosevelt formally dedicated the Smokies park in 1940, in a ceremony aptly held at the Rockefeller Memorial at Newfound Gap, which straddles the Tennessee/North Carolina state line.

The ancient Great Smokies, weathered and worn over millions of years, are nowhere near the highest mountains on the continent. In fact, they are not quite the loftiest mountains in the southern Appalachians, edged out by the Black Mountain range northeast of

Asheville, even if the Smokies do have sixteen summits that exceed six thousand feet. But surely, the Smokies—so named because of the soft, bluish haze on ridges stretching to the horizon—rank among the loveliest and most interesting anywhere. They are favored by a remarkable biodiversity, owing mostly to copious precipitation, elevation and exposure variations, and remnants of the most recent ice age. In Great Smoky Mountains National Park, one can find a couple of historic maintained balds, or treeless summits, but no timberline. More notably, the diversity of trees and plants from the lowest elevations below one thousand feet to the highest well above six thousand is similar to what is found along the entire twenty-two-hundred-mile Appalachian Trail, which extends from north Georgia to central Maine. The park's variety of fauna is impressive as well, ranging from large animals such as elk and black bear to much smaller, often-seen species such as the red squirrel. The Smokies' rich diversity of life (more than nineteen thousand species have been documented in the park), scenic beauty, and compelling human history all contribute to the appeal of the park, which attracted a record 11.3 million visitors in 2016 to make it easily the most heavily visited of our fifty-nine national parks. Not surprisingly, some park roads are clogged with traffic during peak visitor times, as are some parking areas, including those at Newfound Gap and Clingmans Dome.

One reason for the heavy visitation of Great Smoky Mountains National Park is its accessibility via automobile. Not only is the park, with its multiple entrances, within reasonable driving distance of large cities such as Atlanta, Charlotte, and Nashville, it also is traversed by a major highway: U.S. 441, known as Newfound Gap Road within the park. Although winter weather conditions often force temporary closures, the road otherwise typically remains open to vehicle travel throughout the year. And unlike many of its national park counterparts, the park has never been authorized to charge an entrance fee. Even so, 11.3 million is no small number, regardless of how park visitors arrive or how long they visit. The 2016 visitor count is all the more impressive considering the fact that Newfound Gap Road was closed for ten days in late November and early December because of the historic Chimney Tops 2 fire (see Hike 39).

A much smaller number of people hike or backpack deep into the park's backcountry each year, and even fewer hike in areas far removed from the famed Appalachian Trail (AT) and its roughly seventy miles within the park. For example, a handsome backcountry campsite I've maintained for many years as a Smokies volunteer attracted barely five hundred backpackers in a recent year, according to park statistics, despite being situated just over five trail miles from the heavily traveled Newfound Gap Road. Granted, at five thousand feet the site is often difficult to reach and bitterly cold in the winter, but an average of ten campers per week over an entire year is still an infinitesimal percentage of annual park visitation. Of course, some of the more than one hundred backcountry campsites in the park—even those well off the AT—do receive greater use than the small high-elevation site I maintain. In fact, the number of backcountry campers surpassed one hundred thousand in 2016, a sizable number, but still less than one percent of total park visitation.

Comprising some eight hundred square miles, Great Smoky Mountains National Park has mostly reverted to wilderness since its establishment as a national park during the Great Depression. Penetrating its immense backcountry are some 150 maintained trails and 800 official trail miles, including the 70 miles or so of Appalachian Trail. On most of these trails, it takes only a couple of miles of hiking from the trailhead to achieve a real sense of solitude, at least if one is solo hiking. In much of the backcountry, a hiker or backpacker would never know that the park is visited by an average of about two hundred thousand people per week. Notable exceptions include the Appalachian Trail from Newfound Gap to Charlies Bunion and the recently rehabilitated Alum Cave and Chimney Tops Trails in Tennessee. (Alas, the catastrophic Chimney Tops 2 fire late in 2016 heavily damaged the upper part of Chimney Tops Trail, forcing its closure indefinitely.) Each of these trails offers dramatic vistas and features, and each trailhead is located along Newfound Gap Road, the park's primary auto route. No real surprise, then, that these trails attract large numbers of hikers most anytime their paths are clear of snow and ice or other hazards.

What is now the Smokies' trail system actually developed and evolved over thousands of years. Wildlife and native peoples were the original trailblazers in previous millennia, followed by European settlers, and later still, the logging companies that built numerous rail and logging roads in a frenzy to extract as much timber as possible. Upon creation of the park, the Civilian Conservation Corps (CCC) became heavily involved in trail construction and rehabilitation. In the decades since CCC work ended, many other groups and individuals have joined park-service personnel in reconstructing and maintaining trails. Obviously, the trail work done during the past eighty-plus years has been driven by recreational values consistent with those of a national park, rather than the utilitarian ones that continued well into the twentieth century. Consequently, hikers

usually find Smokies' trails well graded and free of major obstacles.

Partly as a result of this modern trail ethic, one is hard pressed to find a trail in the Smokies that isn't enjoyable to hike in good weather. Yes, some trails are rocky, muddy, even eroded in places, despite trail work done specifically to divert water and mitigate the impact of sometimes heavy horse and human traffic. Others suffer from inadequate maintenance, even with park volunteers adopting trails that park-service staff can't cover regularly. And some paths do not feature commanding views, lovely waterfalls, or striking geologic formations. But all offer a story of some sort and a green refuge from civilization, an opportunity to reconnect with the natural world in ecosystems of exceptional diversity. And most of them can be hiked nearly any time of year, though the lengthy spring and fall seasons probably hold the greatest allure for most hikers.

Even deep into the park's backcountry, hikers can encounter evidence of former human activity, including old CCC camps that numbered about two dozen. (One backcountry campsite, at a former CCC camp on Forney Creek, even has the acronym for its name.) Chimney ruins, rusted cable, and domestic plantings can be seen along some trails. But the backcountry's most prominent and poignant reminders of human habitation are the scores of cemeteries that remain inside the national park. In some cases, the gravesites are starkly marked by fieldstones, revealing no names or dates. The cemeteries, totaling more than 150 according to park archives, provide evidence that the Smokies have largely returned to wilderness only within the past century. The Great Smokies indeed have a lengthy human history, evident also by several dozen historic structures that have been preserved in areas such as Cades Cove, Cataloochee, and Greenbrier. No impact was more dramatic and lasting than that of large-scale logging operations, which sought to remove as much timber from the Smokies as quickly as possible in the late-nineteenth and early twentieth centuries, laying waste to much of the forested landscape.

Other parts of the park betray few signs of civilization—modern or otherwise. Perhaps chief among these is the rugged Raven Fork section above the Qualla Boundary of the Eastern Band of Cherokee Indians. A wild, remote area largely untouched by settlers, or even by the logging industry, the park's Raven Fork drainage gives hikers a real sense of wilderness isolation. In fact, most of it lacks maintained trails, not to mention backcountry campsites. Horace Kephart's oft-quoted "back of beyond" phrase fits the Raven Fork area as much as any part of the park.

The terrain of the Smokies is such that park trails typically follow two kinds of natural features: ridges and streams. (The park has well over two thousand miles of the latter—but no natural lakes.) Generally speaking, the trails now pierce densely forested areas that in previous centuries were either logged or cleared for homesteads. How dense? Even thirty years ago, a four-day backpacking trip that my wife, Karen, and I completed in sunny June weather along the North Shore of Fontana Lake yielded no long-range views, except for those atop a nearly mile-high peak known as High Rocks, along remote Welch Ridge. With the logger's ax long since halted by the national park, the blue sky was mostly obscured by lush summer foliage. Today, approximately 95 percent of the park is forested, of which about 25 percent is old growth.

The trails that mostly follow streams are found in various watersheds that reach down from the Smokies' crest, a spine that continuously exceeds an elevation of five thousand feet for more than thirty miles. On the North Carolina side west of Balsam Mountain, several roughly parallel watersheds, separated by high ridges,

carry water that eventually flows into man-made Fontana Lake, which was created by damming the Little Tennessee River in the early 1940s. The watersheds on the Tennessee side, however, aren't quite as neatly aligned. On either side of the great crest, the rushing streams that one often hears when setting out on trails in the Smokies generally have tumbled from the park's highest elevations, from areas that are essentially temperate rain forests. For example, the source of Cooper Creek, which empties into the Tuckasegee River at Ela, North Carolina, is a clear, cold, reliable spring that emerges about seventy-five yards downhill from the Newton Bald backcountry campsite, which sits at five thousand feet in elevation.

As one would expect, Smokies' trails that mostly follow ridges often yield stunning long-range vistas, especially when the deciduous trees are bare. Some of these trails such as The Boulevard, which never dips below an elevation of fifty-five hundred feet, feature spruce-fir forests. Others, including the somewhat lower-elevation Thomas Divide and Cataloochee Divide Trails, are heavily populated by northern hardwood trees with thick foliage from May into October. But particularly on Cataloochee Divide, which roughly forms the park's southeastern boundary, several breaks in the trees afford superb views of distant mountains, regardless of the season.

Other park trails have impressive, if not daunting, elevation gains over relatively few miles. A prime example is Baxter Creek Trail, in the Big Creek section of the park near where Interstate 40 knifes through the rugged Pigeon River Gorge. In slightly more than 6 miles, the trail climbs from about 1,700 feet in elevation at Big Creek to the 5,842-foot-high summit of Mount Sterling. But in terms of ecosystems and vegetation zones, the hike from start to summit is akin to traveling several hundred miles north. And even on a one-day trip, the variation in weather can be dramatic, as I can attest to from day hikes to Mount Sterling that I completed in previous years during the months of June and November.

Most trails in the Smokies, however, are not nearly as strenuous as Baxter Creek Trail. Indian Creek Trail, for example, climbs almost imperceptibly over most of its four-mile course on a graded roadbed from Deep Creek Trail to Martins Gap Trail, which does do some serious climbing. Thus, anyone inclined to hike a few miles into the backcountry can find a trail on either the North Carolina or Tennessee side of the park that isn't terribly demanding. Perhaps one result of *Smokies Chronicle* will be to inspire some park visitors not predisposed to hiking to consider an easy-to-moderate hike. The rewards can be great, just as I expected them to be during my year of hiking several hundred miles in the park. In any event, I hope *Smokies Chronicle* sparks a deeper appreciation of a truly distinctive and endlessly charming national park, not to mention one of exceptional beauty and biodiversity.

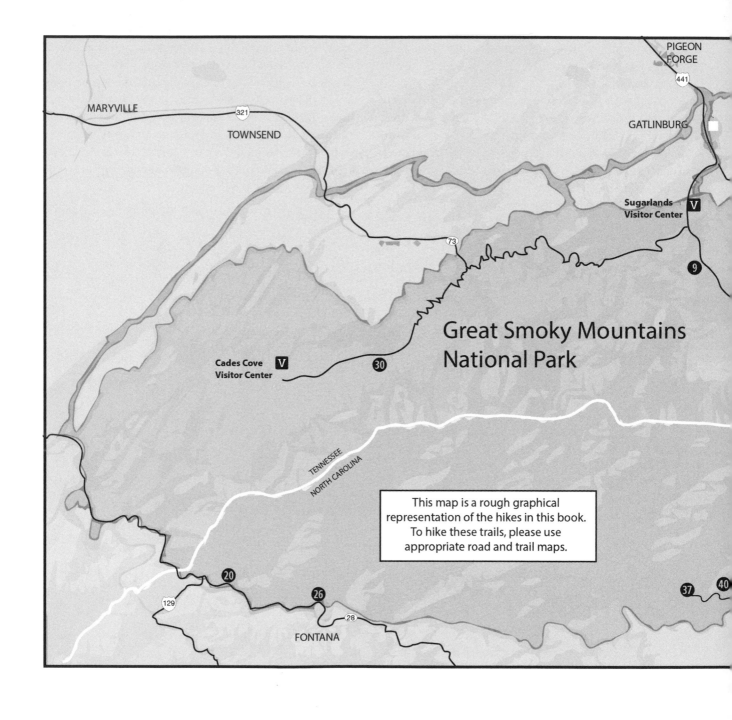

PIGEON FORGE

MARYVILLE

TOWNSEND

321

GATLINBURG

Sugarlands
Visitor Center

9

73

Cades Cove
Visitor Center

30

Great Smoky Mountains
National Park

TENNESSEE
NORTH CAROLINA

This map is a rough graphical
representation of the hikes in this book.
To hike these trails, please use
appropriate road and trail maps.

20

129

26

28

37

40

FONTANA

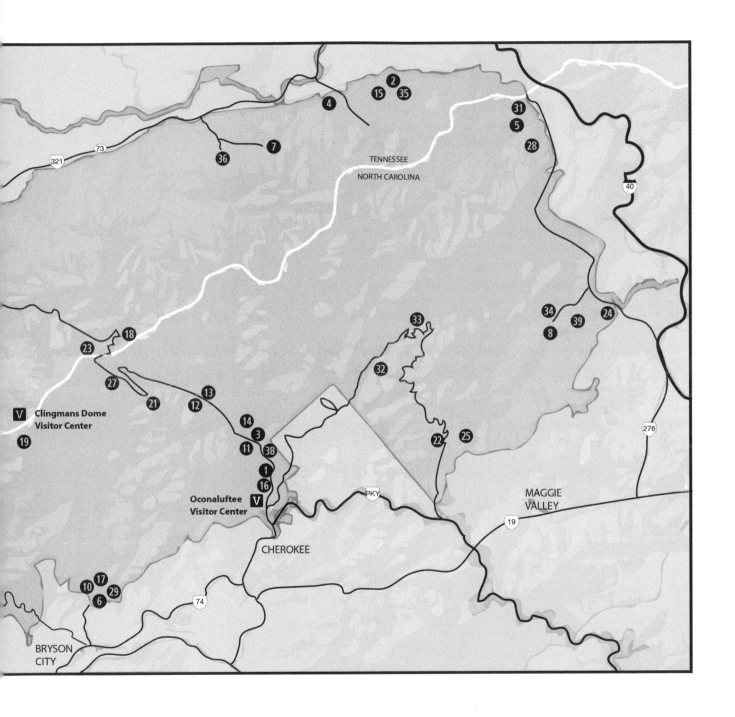

There are no words that can tell the hidden spirit of the wilderness, that can reveal its mystery, its melancholy, and its charm.

—Theodore Roosevelt

Hike 1

At Rest Beyond the Mill

New Year's Day
Trails: **Mingus Creek,**
   Cemetery Spur
Trailhead weather
   conditions: 44 degrees,
   overcast, calm
Round-trip miles hiked: 4.4

January can be a fine time to hike in Great Smoky Mountains National Park, even for those of us who typically favor warm weather. Kindly note use of the word *can*, as the month is often not so fine for hiking in the park. But most years, the Smokies' lower elevations do feature several dry days in January when high temperatures push toward fifty or above and trails are generally free of snow and ice, if not mud. Such are the relatively mild days an antsy warm-weather hiker seizes with a certain urgency. And so it is when son Rob and I set out the day after my sixty-fourth birthday to hike Mingus Creek Trail. The trailhead is located across the creek from the venerable Mingus Mill, thereby launching my year of hiking. This will be one of the few occasions during the year when I am not hiking solo, and partly because of that fact, I decide it is OK for us to hike off-trail for a short distance. On trail or off, I am eager to discover what adventures 2016 will bring in the Great Smoky Mountains.

A half-century after it was built in 1886, Mingus Mill was one of the first historic structures restored after the park was established. Using a cast-iron turbine, rather than a waterwheel, the mill could custom grind grains such as corn, wheat, and rye much faster than other gristmills operating at the time. Restored in the 1980s by the nonprofit Great Smoky Mountains Association, which currently operates it, the mill still produces cornmeal and wheat flour for sale to the public. A couple of hundred yards upstream from the mill, Mingus Creek Trail passes a sluice that diverts creek water to a wooden flume and penstock utilized in powering the turbine. On this gray January day, the mill is silent—closed for the winter—though the creek is anything but silent as it rushes toward Newfound Gap Road and the Oconaluftee River.

Speaking of the river, the lower half of Mingus Creek Trail was not indicated on park trail maps for several years, ostensibly because trail traffic had a harmful impact on the Oconaluftee-area water supply. Though the lower part remains off-limits to horses, hikers now have the green light to hike the trail for its entire 5.8-mile course, starting at the upper end of the Mingus Mill parking area. Good that they do, for it's a scenic route whose character changes greatly from its trailhead at just over two thousand feet in elevation to its terminus at Newton Bald Trail, where the elevation exceeds five thousand feet on the shoulder of the former bald that is now heavily forested.

On this outing, however, Rob and I do not intend to hike the entire length of Mingus Creek Trail, which would be about 11½ miles round-trip, what with the relatively limited amount of daylight available so soon after the winter solstice. Instead, we plan to take a slight detour off the lower section of the main trail, a detour that actually continues to follow Mingus Creek itself to a destination that, like the mill, holds quite a bit of human history.

I first hiked the lower part of Mingus Creek Trail in the early 1980s, in May as I recall. By mid-spring, the foliage was predictably thick and green, and the hiking conditions somewhat muggy and buggy. Today's hike, with winter finally having arrived in the Great Smokies after a freakishly mild and wet December, provides a rather stark contrast to that spring day. As Rob and I proceed up the trail, the woods around us are at rest

with the stillness of January. Several weeks will elapse before the forest again begins to stir with life. The winter silence is broken only by the swiftly flowing Mingus Creek, still swollen after a rainy few months even in the wake of a dry previous day. In fact, the trail itself, which follows an old roadbed along the creek, is not only muddy but also framed near the trailhead by rivulets on either side. If not for foot logs and bridges—though even more slippery than usual—we could not make it very far up Mingus Creek, which is churning and foaming with white water from December downpours.

Winter hiking in the Smokies is not all palettes of brown and gray, as Rob and I observe on this first day of the year. Mosses, ferns, and rhododendron (or laurel, as some old-timers still call it) add splashes of color as we continue up Mingus Creek Trail. On a dry ridge to the north—visible from the trail only in winter—we see the green of several pine trees scattered among the gray hardwoods. But, of course, there's nothing like the profusion of green and other colors that spring will deliver.

Just south of the trail, a high ridge, rising above four thousand feet, separates the park from the Qualla Boundary of the Eastern Band of Cherokee Indians. We pass an old firing range for law-enforcement training before we reach a trail junction. Piggybacked by North Carolina's Mountains-to-Sea Trail as it works toward towering Clingmans Dome, Mingus Creek Trail veers to the left, actually following Madcap Branch instead of Mingus Creek. A wooden sign bearing a single word—CEMETERY—directs us to the right, along the creek itself, and that's the route we choose. With the creek still roiling, slippery foot logs and bridges fortunately provide safe crossings as the trail gradually climbs toward the cemetery.

We continue up the side trail, somewhat surprised to meet two other hikers coming down it on such a quiet winter day. After hiking less than a mile from the junction with Mingus Creek Trail, we arrive at a rock outcrop and a second cemetery sign, pointing to another short side trail that begins between two massive boulders. There's a bit more climbing to do before we reach the cemetery, located on a knoll high above Mingus Creek. There's no chance whatsoever that the creek will flood this final resting place for more than forty souls.

The cemetery lies in a large clearing, with a stunning wintertime view of the soaring ridge that Mingus Creek Trail follows toward its junction with Newton Bald Trail. It is truly a lovely, peaceful setting for a cemetery. In contrast, the gravesites themselves are starkly marked, with fieldstones instead of cut-granite headstones. Only the stone for the gravesite of Mrs. Polly Mathis has a named etched into it that can be read. The carving is still somewhat difficult to decipher, but we decide that it looks as if she lived from 1888 to 1934, the year the park was established. Surely these gravesites betray the hardscrabble lives these settlers must have lived well into the twentieth century.

About a mile north of the cemetery is a little-known peak of not quite four thousand feet named Mount Stand Watie. The mountain's namesake was a Cherokee chief and later Confederate brigadier general, whose older brother was Elias Boudinot, editor of the *Cherokee Phoenix* newspaper. In 1835, Stand Watie was a signer of the treaty that led to the tragic removal of the Cherokee to Oklahoma Territory. After leaving the cemetery, we decide to follow a faint trail—sometimes called a manway—along the creek to see if we can make it to the western flank of Mount Stand Watie. But after one hundred yards or so, we're stymied when the unmaintained trail apparently crosses the rushing high water of Mingus Creek. After scrambling through undergrowth for roughly another one hundred yards in an effort to find a safe fording of the creek, we abandon the quest—Stand Watie will stand alone on this winter day, nearly a mile from our stopping point. We thrash our way back toward the cemetery, to the open path that leads us back to Mingus Creek Trail. The walking becomes easy again, except for the caution required on the logs and bridges crossing Mingus Creek.

Near the trailhead, there's one more cemetery to look for, just slightly off-trail. If the lives of those who are buried farther up the creek were difficult, the ones laid to rest at this cemetery were all the more so, for it's a slave cemetery. We leave Mingus Creek Trail, going away from the creek, on a slightly worn path to our left near the parking lot. Although we locate a relatively flat area that looks like a final resting place, we're unable to find even a rudimentary marker or headstone. If we have identified the correct location of the cemetery, there's no evidence of it above ground. (*Footnote*: Later in the year, I located four graves, marked by fieldstones, in a small plot above the upper end of the parking area. These are likely the graves we were looking for on New Year's Day.)

It's been a good, if unspectacular, first hike of the year. The trail, following one of the Smokies' many lovely streams coursing through deep folds in the mountains, is an example of a rewarding park trail that doesn't require a major investment of time and energy. It also reflects the fact that long before the Smokies became a great national park, human inhabitants helped shape the history of this rugged landscape.

Hike 2

New Territory in Tennessee

January 7
Trail: Gabes Mountain
Trailhead weather
   conditions: 32 degrees,
   sunny, calm
Round-trip miles hiked: 9.8

After starting the year with a hike in North Carolina, it's time for an excursion on the Tennessee side of the Great Smokies. From my home in Asheville, the most accessible trailheads in Tennessee are found in the Cosby section of the park, even when the Foothills Parkway off Interstate 40 is closed because of snow and ice. Although the Cosby area was once labeled the moonshine capital of the world, other locations in the southern and central Appalachians have shared the same title. But true to its billing, as I approach an I-40 exit near Cosby, a couple of signs tout MOONSHINE and FREE SAMPLES, obviously for the intrepid traveler.

On a more sober note, Cosby trails, which start at elevations below twenty-five hundred feet, will no doubt offer several good hiking possibilities during the balance of the winter. On this bright January day, I opt to hike Gabes Mountain Trail, a footpath I've never set boot upon. It's a trail the Civilian Conservation Corps completed in 1934, the year the park was established. But today, it offers me completely new territory, always an appealing prospect in the Great Smoky Mountains.

Starting at a trailhead across the road from the Cosby

picnic ground, I aim for the Sugar Cove backcountry campsite, a destination not quite five miles out. With a mid-morning start and a total elevation gain of less than fifteen hundred feet, Sugar Cove seems a reasonable goal for the day. Gabes Mountain Trail actually continues for nearly two miles past the campsite, but I don't plan to hike the entire distance today. Along the way, there's a short side trip to Hen Wallow Falls, with a viewing spot reached via a spur trail of about three hundred yards. As I set out on the main trail, my aging Jeep is the only vehicle in the spacious parking lot. Surely, there will be plenty of solitude on this winter hike, at least initially.

A frosting of snow is scattered on the ground, as well as on some logs and stream boulders, as I embark on the trail about 10 o'clock. As for the trail itself, the surface is mostly frozen and often crunchy to the step. But with a benevolent sun lifting the morning's subfreezing temperatures, it's shaping up as a fine day for a hike on the northern slopes of the Smokies' crest. Upon my return in the afternoon, the dusting of snow will have mostly vanished, along with most of the morning ice, forming muddy tracks in many places. The freeze-thaw process so common on winter days at this latitude and altitude is clearly at work on this second outing of the year.

Near the start, someone has scrawled *2016* in the snow that lingers on a large fallen tree, welcoming the new year with a benign patch of fleeting snow graffiti. Farther up the trail, some unusually large holly trees stand among the hemlocks and hardwoods. Just under a mile out, water from a branch of Crying Creek rushes through two small culverts, placed at either end of a handsome rock bridge. Despite a generally dry start to January, most streams and their tributaries are still running high from periodic heavy rains over the past few months.

A low-slung sun continues rising above the Smok-ies' divide to my left as I proceed up the trail. When the trail swings away from Crying Creek in rounding a bend, the silence of the woods is unbroken except for the *tap-tap-tap* of a hardworking woodpecker. I look up at the cluster of trees where the sound is originating, but I fail to spot the noisemaker. Slightly farther along the trail, I look back and see prominent Mount Cammerer, the northeastern rampart of the Smokies' crest before the divide falls off sharply to the Pigeon River Gorge.

Soon I encounter my first real trail hazard of the new year: a sheet of ice extending across the trail for several feet. From a seep coming out of a sizable boulder, a daunting sheet has formed in the wake of a blast of Arctic air that blew in earlier in the week. With a hiking pole providing some stability, I tread gingerly, mindful that a spill could pose a major problem as I'm roughly two miles from any form of civilization. But I manage to make it across without incident. Shortly afterward, I'm rewarded with a fine view to the north of English Mountain, a massif that rises above the Tennessee foothills to an elevation exceeding thirty-six hundred feet. I proceed unimpeded again.

About halfway to Sugar Cove, water gushes from a rock face, but fortunately doesn't create an ice sheet across the trail. Jutting out a few feet above ground from the underside of a log, twin ice sculptures resemble clear fish hanging from a line. Amid rising temperatures, both formations will crash to the ground before my return a few hours later.

I reach a sunny, open cove (what is called a bowl in the West) at about the three-mile mark. Soon I enter another cove, featuring a tributary and impressively large hemlocks and poplars. Farther along, yet another branch shimmers in the midday sun as I descend toward it on the trail. I finally spot my first bird of the day, a junco, before the trail crosses a dry creek bed—somewhat of a surprise considering the recent deluges.

The trail mostly flattens, a rarity in these mountains, for the final 1½ miles before Sugar Cove. A large uprooted tree just off trail has an exposed root ball as large as a bedroom, creating a crater-sized hole in the ground. Nearby, I see a few patches of mountain oat grass along the trail, as well as a small boggy area.

Well into the afternoon, I reach the Sugar Cove campsite just beyond a rock-hop crossing of Greenbrier Creek. Open, level places to pitch even a small tent are difficult to come by here, but the beauty of this camp along the creek more than compensates for that deficiency. I spread out on a boulder for lunch, warmed by the sun at my back. By now temperatures have climbed into the forties, even though a few clouds have gathered in the vivid blue sky.

A few minutes later, I think I hear voices above the sounds of Greenbrier Creek. Soon that thinking is confirmed as I see two day hikers approaching from the direction of Maddron Bald Trail to the west. They continue past the campsite and creek, toward where I started my hike a few hours earlier. Within a couple of minutes, I once again have this lovely spot to myself.

After lunch, the main order of business on the way back to my car is the short side trip to Hen Wallow Falls, which I chose to bypass earlier. Even with its longtime popularity, I'm surprised on my return trip to encounter about a dozen hikers between the falls area and the parking lot. Unfortunately, one hiker decides to relieve herself right in the middle of the trail. I stop in my tracks and dutifully turn away after spotting her, waiting a couple of minutes before proceeding down the trail. Is it asking too much to expect hikers to answer the call at least a few yards off-trail?

As expected, Hen Wallow Falls proves well worth the effort required to descend the generally steep, rocky, narrow spur to a spot among a jumble of rocks where the falls are best viewed. In addition to torrents of water, the falls feature giant icicles and a couple of large hummocks of ice on this winter day. The spilling water crashes amid the rocks, providing quite a show, especially with the current high water levels. Hen Wallow Falls reminds me of the less accessible and less visited Little Creek Falls along Deeplow Gap Trail, in the Deep Creek area of the park. The rushing beauty of the falls lifts the spirit.

After a few minutes, I'm ready for the short walk back to Gabes Mountain Trail and the ensuing two miles to the trailhead. It's been a highly satisfying first hike of the year on the Tennessee side of the Smokies, surpassing even my lofty expectations. If the rest of the brand-new territory I explore in the park proves as pleasurable, I'm in for a terrific year.

Hike 3

Flats, but No Cabin

January 14
Trails: Bradley Fork, Cabin
   Flats, Chasteen Creek
*Trailhead weather
   conditions:* 35 degrees,
   sunny, calm
Round-trip miles hiked: 10.6

The upper part of Smokemont Campground, off New-found Gap Road a few miles north of Cherokee, North Carolina, is deserted as Karen and I walk through it on this winter day. In fact, the entire 142-site campground is basically deserted. A bustling place especially from about mid-June to mid-August, this section of the popular year-round campground is closed to camping during the colder months. But from past experiences, I can almost smell wood smoke and hear children's voices as we continue through the upper loop. Today we're traveling the loop on foot because the section is gated and trailhead parking for Bradley Fork Trail cannot be reached by car. And Bradley Fork is the trail—or more accurately, well-graded jeep road—we need to hike to reach today's destination: the Cabin Flats backcountry campsite via the connecting Cabin Flats Trail. We have no plans to camp in the January elements, however, even if they are relatively benign today.

I have a rather extensive personal history with Smoke-mont, where I've camped several times, and the lower part of Bradley Fork Trail, which I've hiked many times. The most memorable campout occurred when I took our older son, Ben, on his first camping trip shortly after his third birthday. Soon after we pulled into one of the few remaining vacant sites, a black bear showed up looking for an early supper and climbed up on our picnic table. I quickly got Ben into our little Dodge Colt, where we waited till the bear moved on to his next campsite. Fortunately, the intruder did no real harm, except for swiping a couple of Hershey bars and putting a slight dent in our camp stove. The bear paid our campsite another visit at breakfast the next morning but came up empty pawed. Bears do have a strong sense of when and where they might pick off an easy meal, and Smokies picnic areas and campgrounds can offer convenient options.

Once known as Bradleytown, Smokemont has its own history, especially as a prototype logging and sawmill town of the early twentieth century. By the 1920s, Champion Fibre Company had transformed Smokemont into a large-scale operation that during its heyday produced up to forty-five thousand board feet of lumber and pulpwood daily. With its narrow-gauge railroad tracks, post office, commissary, homes, and school now long gone, the only prominent reminder of the bygone Smokemont community is its Baptist church, just downstream from the present-day campground.

Slightly more than a mile out, Bradley Fork Trail is the jumping-off point for Chasteen Creek Trail and its two backcountry campsites, each of which I maintained for several years as an Adopt-a-Campsite volunteer for the park. For the past few years, however, I've focused on the high-elevation Newton Bald site, located just off the sublime upper section of the lengthy Thomas Divide Trail. Before this mid-January day, I hadn't hiked Bradley Fork Trail in a few years and hadn't made it to Cabin Flats in more than twenty. It was time to get reacquainted.

We probably could not have a better January-weather day ahead of us as we reach the trailhead about 11 o'clock. Yes, it's still cold, especially where ridges block the sun, but afternoon temperatures are headed toward the fifties with blue sky and very little wind. We do encounter a couple of patches of trail ice near the start, but they pose little trouble.

The first four miles or so of Bradley Fork Trail—the part of it we're hiking today—mostly hug the fork at creek level. As we follow the Bradley Fork and Cabin Flats Trails, we'll be veering slightly west of due north, stopping a few miles south of the fork's headwaters near the Appalachian Trail and Smokies' crest. Starting at an altitude of about twenty-two hundred feet, our elevation gain will be less than one thousand feet because the route has no major ascents. Along the way, especially with the high water levels, we'll see many beautiful cascades and pools, as the winter sunlight dances upon Bradley Fork.

As we proceed, the lower part of the trail is rockier and ruttier than I recall from the dozens of times I've hiked it en route to backcountry volunteer work. Although the trail does receive a great deal of horse traffic during the warmer months, perhaps a bigger factor in its rougher condition is the tremendous amount of rainfall the Smokies received over the past few months. But the old road that Bradley Fork Trail follows for its first four miles remains easy to walk, with no significant obstacles.

Soon after we clear Chasteen Creek on a sturdy wooden bridge, the trail reaches the junction with Chasteen Creek Trail, which gains about two thousand feet on its four-mile course before ending at a trail junction on Hughes Ridge. We catch a glimpse of two hikers a hundred yards or so ahead of us, a couple we'll overtake a half-mile later where Smokemont Loop Trail exits left to cross Bradley Fork. If you're skittish about foot logs, the one spanning Bradley Fork probably is one to avoid. It's not only fairly long, but it also has a wooden railing that leans quite a bit upstream. Nonetheless, the loop is a popular 5½-mile hike out of Smokemont Campground.

We continue to climb gradually on Bradley Fork Trail. About 1½ miles beyond the Smokemont Loop junction, we finally cross the fork on a pair of wide bridges that take the trail across an island in the stream. Another half-mile or so up the trail, just past where hard-charging Taywa Creek empties into Bradley Fork, two more day hikers are sitting on the final bridge we'll cross before meeting up with Cabin Flats Trail.

At four miles, we arrive at the large road turn-around that marks the beginning of Cabin Flats Trail. The trail is located to the right of a large downed tree and a lengthy piece of rope that stretches between two standing trees. Farther to the right, Bradley Fork Trail doubles back on itself above the fork as it begins its first significant climb, gaining about two thousand feet in elevation before reaching Hughes Ridge in fewer than 3½ miles. For our part, we're happy to pick up Cabin Flats Trail at this point, especially with our destination only about one mile away.

Fewer than one hundred yards past the turnaround, we cross Bradley Fork for the final time, on a narrow old truss bridge. Just beyond the bridge, we take a sharp left to continue on Cabin Flats Trail. This is a lovely spot by the fork, enhanced by a small waterfall and pool just downstream from the bridge. The trail then switches back to the right, taking us toward its junction with Dry Sluice Gap Trail.

Just before the Dry Sluice junction, we reach the somewhat curiously named Tennessee Branch, which originates near the Smokies' divide but is still some distance south of the Tennessee/North Carolina state line. Fortunately, the foot log spanning the branch is relatively short, because it has no handrail. If the log were icy, we might be turning around ourselves at this point.

But we carefully negotiate the log and continue to the junction of Cabin Flats/Dry Sluice Gap Trails, where a trail sign notes we're just over four miles from the Appalachian Trail.

Past the junction, Cabin Flats Trail levels before descending to the end of the line at Cabin Flats backcountry campsite, an especially handsome site in a broad flat area hard by Bradley Fork. The mouth of Cabin Branch is across the fork, but if there were ever a cabin in these parts there's no evidence of it now. In any case, the flats provide many nice spots for us to choose from to sit and enjoy lunch after a couple of hours of hiking.

Soon we leave Cabin Flats for the return trip to Smokemont. As we climb the trail above the flats, Long Ridge is prominent to our left before we begin the descent back to Bradley Fork, just beyond the Dry Sluice junction. A highlight on the return trip is a sunny spot on our left, where we decide to rest on a wooden bench near a hitching post. Almost immediately after departing this open area, we're back on a damp, shaded section of trail, where it feels as if the temperature has suddenly dropped at least five degrees. Later on, as Karen continues on Bradley Fork Trail, I decide to take a quick side trip of about two hundred yards to the Lower Chasteen campsite that I've worked many times as a volunteer but haven't visited in the past few years. Not surprisingly, the camp is deserted.

A fine day in the Bradley Fork Valley ends with our seeing several wild turkeys near our car, followed by a sighting from the car of a couple dozen elk in the broad Oconaluftee Valley. But much as we enjoyed the relatively mild, blue-sky day, we will appreciate it all the more the next day, when a steady cold rain soaks the mountains for most of a miserable-weather day. A familiar adage is strongly reinforced for us: *carpe diem.*

Hike 4

Calm after the Storm

January 28
Trails: Maddron Bald,
  Albright Grove Loop
*Trailhead weather
  conditions:* 33 degrees,
  overcast, calm
Round-trip miles hiked: 7.8

After a fast start out of the gate with three excellent hikes during the first two weeks of January, the reality of winter in the Great Smoky Mountains hits full force. Does it ever! A major storm blasts the mountains January 22-23, making hiking problematic at best for several days, especially on the North Carolina side of the Smokies. Skiing, snowboarding, snowshoeing—all would be OK in accessible areas of the mountains in the aftermath of the storm. But such is not the case for hiking, as it will take some time even for low-elevation trails to thaw and for roads to trailheads to reopen. And melting snow and ice spell mostly muddy trails, even when they can be reasonably hiked again.

More new territory in Tennessee is the goal when favorable trail and road conditions coincide with a schedule opening. And not just any territory, because I have in mind one of the park's exceptional places: Albright Grove, in the Cosby area. The grove harbors majestic old-growth trees that I am long overdue to visit. As with Cabin Flats Trail a couple of weeks prior, I will reach Albright Grove Loop Trail after a longer hike on another trail. On this excursion, the longer route follows Maddron Bald Trail, which meets up with the loop trail after about three miles. In turn, Albright Grove Loop Trail makes its way through the grove for only about three-fourths mile—a decidedly memorable three-fourths.

A couple of nomenclature notes: Maddron Bald is

named for a nineteenth-century Tennessean, the Reverend Lawson Maddron, who lived near the bald. Albright Grove, in contrast, is named for Horace Albright, a native Californian, who never lived anywhere near the grove or the Great Smoky Mountains.

Why name the area for Albright? Perhaps a better question would be, why not name it for Albright? The first assistant director of the National Park Service, Albright served as its second director from 1929 to 1933, during a period of intense negotiations for critical land acquisitions that helped form the park. He also is generally credited with shooting down an ill-conceived plan to construct a road along the entire crest of the Smokies—a much longer route than the seven-mile-long skyway that today runs from Newfound Gap to the southern flank of Clingmans Dome. The predominant wilderness character of the Appalachian Trail, as it tracks about seventy miles through the Smokies, would have been lost forever had the road been built. So, yes, an old-growth grove in the Great Smokies named for Albright seems eminently appropriate.

Footnote: After his highly productive—if relatively short—stint as director, Albright left the National Park Service to become a captain of commerce, joining the United States Potash Company. He worked there until he retired as company president in the mid-1950s. But Albright left an indelible mark on the park service during the years that Stephen Mather, its first director, and he largely shaped it.

Maddron Bald Trail—its lower section, at least—is another enduring example of Civilian Conservation Corps handiwork of the 1930s. It's a well-constructed, well-graded roadbed that remains in good condition and easy to hike, at least as far as Albright Grove. Finding the trailhead, however, isn't so easy, even though it's just a short distance from U.S. 321.

After driving to Tennessee past rime-laden trees, framing Interstate 40 in the Pigeon River Gorge, I stop at an attractive privately owned campground on U.S. 321, west of Cosby. I offer to pay to park there for a few hours, as I had read in a couple of hiking guides that it may not be safe to park at the Maddron Bald trailhead. But the friendly fellow doing outside maintenance refuses to accept even a small payment, insisting that I leave my car there at no charge. Still unsure of how far I actually am from the trailhead, I decide, despite his hospitality, to get back in the car and look for the trailhead via the elusive Baxter Road, which turns out to be just east of the campground. I turn onto the road, driving for less than one half-mile past what seems to be a mix of year-round and vacation homes, before seeing a large brown sign, directing me to take a sharp right to reach the Maddron Bald trailhead. About one hundred yards down this unmarked road, there's an empty parking area on the left with space for three or four cars just outside a park-service gate. I decide not to expect trouble and proceed to park my car there as the unpaved area's lone vehicle, cautionary trail guides notwithstanding. Upon my return a few hours later, I feel vindicated when I find my car as I left it. Perhaps I'm just fortunate, or perhaps the warnings are outdated or overblown. Either way, of course, I'm happy to find my car undisturbed.

But enough about cars and parking; the trail's the thing. And Maddron Bald Trail proves to be a delightful route. As I head up the trail from the gate, I see a couple of private residences to my left, just outside the park boundary, before coming to a tiny nineteenth-century home in a glade to my right, less than three-fourths mile up the trail. Outside the short front door, a park-service sign informs me that this is the Willis Baxter Cabin, constructed of chestnut before the twentieth-century blight.

The sign also notes that the one-room cabin, which has fewer than three hundred square feet of living space, was built about 1889—coincidentally the same year construction began on the 175,000-square-foot Biltmore House east of the Smokies in Asheville, North Carolina. Literally hundreds of Baxter cabins could fit inside the mammoth Biltmore House, the French Renaissance–style chateau that took six years to complete.

A half-mile or so up the trail, I come to an expansive trail intersection. To my left is Gabes Mountain Trail, most of which I traveled a few weeks earlier by hiking from its opposite end. To my right is Old Settlers Trail, which snakes its way for nearly sixteen miles to Greenbrier Cove. As for Maddron Bald Trail, it continues straight ahead. By now, the morning fog and clouds have dissipated, giving way to a gorgeous blue sky, broken by just a few high, thin clouds. I follow the January sun south, in the direction of Greenbrier Pinnacle, as I work toward my highly anticipated destination of Albright Grove.

Although Maddron Bald Trail narrows in a few places above the intersection, it's still wide enough for a couple of hikers to walk abreast. But walking abreast doesn't come into play today, as I'm hiking alone. In fact, this will be the first hike of the year on which I don't see another mortal being. Solitude, as well as quietude, will be the order of the day.

Another 1½ miles or so up the trail, I reach the first major stream crossing of the day, as Maddron Bald Trail reaches churning Indian Camp Creek. Fortunately, the footbridge spanning the creek is sturdy with a good handrail. It's built of two adjoining split logs and has a partial macadam surface. Right after the creek crossing, I encounter a few patches of ice on the trail, but they are easily avoided. Albright Grove isn't far away.

Soon I reach the junction with Albright Grove Loop Trail. I plan to continue on Maddron Bald Trail, sharply veering to the left from here, and pick up the loop trail from its upper end in another one-third mile. But the lure of the grove proves too great to resist, even briefly, and I decide to proceed straight ahead on the loop trail, which meanders between Dunn and Indian Camp Creeks at an elevation of about thirty-two hundred feet.

The grove, once owned but never logged by Champion Fibre Company, is magnificent—a tree hugger's paradise. I walk and stand among giants here, in a virgin forest that includes enormous yellow poplars, maples, silverbells, Fraser magnolias, and yes, some large Eastern hemlocks that have not yet succumbed to the exotic hemlock woolly adelgid. The biggest of the big is a yellow poplar with a circumference exceeding twenty-five feet. As I amble through the grove, I have the sense of being in an outdoor cathedral; it truly is a place of wonder in these mountains. All too soon, I reach the loop's upper junction with Maddron Bald Trail and decide I must backtrack on Albright Grove Loop Trail, so that I can get one more look at the grove's stately sentinels. I stop for a late lunch in the afternoon sun about halfway along the loop, alone with these giants of the forest.

After completing an out-and-back trip through the grove, I decide to hike the one-third mile up the Maddron Bald Trail to its upper junction with Albright Grove Loop Trail. I'm glad that I do, as that short section of the Maddron Bald Trail yields some fine wintertime views of the grand grove to the right. Even after revisiting this farther junction, I'm still just slightly more than three miles from the original trailhead, with plenty of daylight remaining.

I start back on Maddron Bald Trail toward its trailhead, wondering why it has taken me so many years to hike these two rewarding trails. Now that I know the way to the hard-to-find trailhead, I'm guessing it won't be long before I return. It's hard to imagine a better way, or better January conditions, to wrap up my first month of Smokies hiking.

Hike 5

Super Sunday—on Big Creek

February 7
Trail: Big Creek
Trailhead weather
  conditions: 46 degrees,
  scattered clouds, breezy
Round-trip miles hiked: 10.4

Yes, there's a football game later today involving the home-state team, preceded by elaborate parties and marathon pre-game shows. But on a crisp, blue-sky day in the mountains, the Big Creek section of Great Smoky Mountains National Park beckons. Located on the northeastern edge of the park near the North Carolina/Tennessee border, Big Creek has three relatively low-elevation trailheads that provide good starting points for wintertime hiking.

In contrast with my previous hike, the parking area for Big Creek Trail isn't particularly difficult to find. But the driving route to it from Asheville is hardly a straight shot. In fact, getting there requires driving a short distance into Tennessee to Interstate 40, Exit 451—yes, the exit is 451 miles across Tennessee from I-40's eastbound crossing of the Mississippi River. I then double back on narrow roads to North Carolina, where Big Creek charges out of the park to meet the Pigeon River.

I drive past the Walters hydroelectric plant and the tiny communities of Waterville and Mount Sterling, just outside the park boundary, before reaching the narrow park road that takes me about 1¼ miles to the large parking area that serves day hikers, backpackers, and (in season) picnickers. Not too surprisingly on a fine February day, I find about a dozen cars parked there. Although I will be hiking solo again, no doubt I will encounter quite a few hikers on the trail this time out. Soon, that expectation is confirmed. Among the two dozen or so people I end up seeing at various points are not only the first backpackers of the year, but also the first horseback rider. Big Creek is undeniably a popular place anytime the weather is favorable.

Even in the Smokies' backcountry, which has the characteristics of a wilderness area even if lacking a federal designation as such, man-made additions still seem justified in some places. A good example in the park is the addition of food-storage cable systems at backcountry campsites. The cables provide a much more efficient way of keeping food out of the reach of bears and other animals than the old method of suspending packs and food by using ropes and tree limbs. Although the park's official trail map notes that food cables are installed at all backcountry sites, it still includes instructions on how to safely hang food and packs:

> Select two trees, 10-20 feet apart, with limbs 15 feet high. Using a rock for a weight, toss a rope over a limb on the first tree; tie one end to the pack. Repeat this process with the second tree. Raise the pack about six feet via the first rope and tie it off. Then pull the second rope until the pack is suspended at least 10 feet high and evenly spaced; it must be four feet or more from the nearest limb.

Gee, sounds easy enough—or maybe not. Conversely, the cable systems indeed are easy to operate, as they utilize eyebolts, clips, and hooks to help backpackers safely suspend packs out of the reach of bears.

The food cables are excellent additions to the Smokies' backcountry, as are permanent fire rings, designed to limit and contain open fires at each campsite location.

I note all this because no backcountry campsite warrants these man-made additions more than today's chosen destination: Lower Walnut Bottom, located just over five miles up Big Creek Trail. The beautiful, open area with several attractive tent sites has long been popular not only with backpackers, but also with bears whose activity has prompted a number of temporary campsite closures over the years. Although bears certainly haven't vanished from the area, the food cables have at least made the task of protecting food and backpacks considerably easier.

After arriving at the parking area, I walk the short distance uphill to the trailhead for Big Creek Trail. The path runs about six miles before giving way to Camel Gap Trail, which ascends to the Appalachian Trail. Today I plan to hike only as far as its junction with Low Gap Trail (North Carolina side), which I'll reach after about 5¼ miles. There's a total elevation gain of more than one thousand feet over that distance, but the ascent is so gradual it's not noticed for the most part.

As I set out slightly after noon, a bright blue sky and comfortable hiking weather prevail. Converted from a logging rail line into a roadbed by the Civilian Conservation Corps, the trail initially climbs well above Big Creek, before soon dropping back down to follow the trail mostly near creek level the rest of the way. The walking is easy and pleasant, with only a few wet places. Looming to my left is the soaring Mount Sterling Ridge, attaining an elevation more than four thousand feet higher than the lower section of Big Creek. There's no chance the temperature is in the mid-forties up there today.

A mile or so up the trail, amid a boulder field off-trail on the ridge to my right, is a natural formation known as the Rock House, easily capable of providing shelter from a storm with its essentially flat twenty-five-foot "ceiling." With no storm in sight today, I bypass the faint side trail that leads to the house and continue another three-fourths mile on Big Creek Trail to a sunny spot near a deep pool, where I sit on a streamside boulder to enjoy a snack. A bit farther along the trail, I get a glimpse of the lovely Mouse Creek Falls on the opposite side of the creek, but I decide to pause only briefly as other hikers have stopped at the viewing spot.

After another one-fourth mile, I reach the first creek crossing by way of a wide wooden bridge. Big Creek narrows and rushes under the bridge amid a jumble of rocks before collecting itself in a large, beautiful, relatively calm pool just downstream. After crossing the bridge, I mostly lose the abundant sunlight I've enjoyed to this point, as the ridge on the southern side of Big Creek essentially obscures the sun even early in the afternoon. Among the boulders in the creek is a big rock, shaped almost perfectly like a pyramid with its pointed top. Soon I reach an area of numerous downed trees, felled by a storm rather than logging, and a nice resting place between a hitching post and the stream.

After about 4½ miles, I come to a concrete ford across Flint Rock Cove Creek. Rather than take a couple of steps in ankle-deep water, I decide to rock-hop across the creek. Soon I reach a junction on my left with Swallow Fork Trail, which climbs four miles to Mount Sterling Ridge before the second bridge crossing of Big Creek. Just past the bridge, I arrive at the exceptionally attractive Lower Walnut Bottom backcountry campsite. Based upon the number of backpackers I saw earlier who were hiking back to the Big Creek trailhead, about a dozen camped here on the cold preceding night. In fact, one of the tent sites still has campers. Although it and the other sites between the trail and the creek probably are considered prime spots, a large level site on the right side of the trail isn't exactly shabby—it's also near the beautifully cascading Chestnut Cove Creek. But after a short walk up to the Low Gap trailhead, I choose to eat lunch at a sunnier site on the left side of Big Creek Trail. Off-limits to horses—unlike its cousin Upper Walnut Bottom another mile up the trail—Lower Walnut Bottom is understandably a favored site for backpackers.

The afternoon is getting on and it's time for me to hike back to the trailhead, especially since I plan to stop at two wonderful spots on the return trip: Mouse Creek Falls and Midnight Hole. About three miles back down the trail is the striking, if unfortunately named, Mouse Creek Falls, which plummets about fifty feet in making a dramatic entry into Big Creek. The falls are especially stunning when water levels are high, as they are today. Slightly more than a half-mile farther downstream, I walk off-trail to admire the more romantically named Midnight Hole, an unusually large and deep pool just below the spot where Big Creek squeezes between two large boulders. Because it's a postcard-pretty spot that's difficult to leave, I linger for a few minutes before continuing on Big Creek Trail.

Although major logging operations began on the Big Creek watershed in the late-nineteenth century and continued well into the twentieth, the forest continues to recover nicely. The clear, rushing stream creates many pleasant scenes as it courses between the towering forested ridges, begging a visit most anytime of the year. But the timing of this early February outing is especially opportune, as frigid weather and numerous snow showers will gain a stronghold across the Smokies over the next several days. Yes, it's still winter.

Hike 6

Five Trails, One Loop

February 18
Trails: Thomas Divide,
   Indian Creek Motor,
   Deeplow Gap, Indian
   Creek, Deep Creek
*Trailhead weather
   conditions:* 39 degrees,
   sunny, calm
Round-trip miles hiked: 9.9

"Something for everyone" is an overused phrase and, perhaps, an often inaccurate one. But when it comes to recreational opportunities in the Deep Creek area of the park, the expression seems to fit quite nicely.

Deep Creek offers several hiking (and strolling) options, including long and short loops featuring some of the park's loveliest waterfalls. Other popular activities include backpacking, fly fishing, horseback riding, frontcountry camping, picnicking, jogging, and even some cycling—a rarity on trails in the Smokies. But perhaps Deep Creek's chief recreational claim to fame is its tubing, especially from about mid-June to mid-August. On hot summer days when water levels are favorable, Deep Creek is clearly the place to be for tubing in the Smokies—what with its bouncy, bracing run of a mile or so from the mouth of Indian Creek to the park boundary.

Predictably on this cool February morning, there are no tubists (not to be confused with cubists) in sight. In fact, there are very few humans, period, and just a couple of vehicles in the spacious day-use parking area. At the picnic ground, the lone discernable activity is a doe poking around one of the tables. As for the campground, the only thing humming—well, blaring—is a leaf blower operated by a park employee, even with the campground opening still about seven weeks out.

Although I have been to Deep Creek dozens of times for various purposes, including tubing, today I plan to see a bit of new territory. The idea is to fashion a hiking loop of about ten miles, starting with my walking up Tom Branch Road for about a mile from its Deep Creek bridge. Next, I pick up Thomas Divide Trail for roughly 3¼ miles to its junction with Indian Creek Motor Trail, which I have never hiked before. The latter trail takes me down to three familiar trails that return me to my car in the day-use parking area. Previously, I have done several loop hikes in the Deep Creek area, but this somewhat unconventional loop involving five trails and a road is a first for me.

I discover right away that Tom Branch Road has recently reopened to vehicle traffic, after being closed for several days because of snow and ice. But there isn't much traffic on this Thursday in February; in fact, I encounter just two vehicles on my twenty-minute walk up the road to the Thomas Divide trailhead. By now, the road is mostly thawed, giving way to mud, save for a few icy potholes in the shade. During the winter, the primary benefits of walking the road are the nice views and sounds of Tom Branch to my left, only a short distance from where the branch drops dramatically off the ridge to create a much-admired eighty-foot-high waterfall descending into Deep Creek. As I reach a spot where the road levels from its initially steep climb, I get a glimpse of the distant Smokies' divide, high above the Deep Creek watershed.

Soon I arrive at the trailhead for Thomas Divide Trail, one of the longest paths in the Smokies. The trail follows the crescent-shaped divide for nearly fourteen miles, attaining a mile-high elevation on Nettle Creek Bald, which is within three miles of the trail's northern

terminus at Newfound Gap Road. Here at its southern end, in contrast, the elevation is not much higher than two thousand feet. Along the way, there are two deep gaps: the aptly named Deeplow Gap and Tuskee Gap, a few miles farther north.

Almost immediately after setting out on Thomas Divide Trail, I take a short side trail to my left to the Wiggins-Watson Cemetery. It's perfectly still and quiet as I arrive there, until the *cawk-cawk-cawk* of a crow intrudes, as does the buzz of an airplane shortly thereafter. But the cemetery remains a beautiful, peaceful spot in the late-winter sun, with a nice view of thirty-four-hundred-foot Sharp Top, situated along the park boundary west of Deep Creek. Near the perimeter of the cemetery, a prominent granite marker, chiseled with the words *Together Forever*, marks the final resting places for Jesse W. and Edna M. Watson. Mr. Watson lived from 1915 to 1977; no year of passing is noted for Mrs. Watson, born in 1922. One might surmise that she has not yet departed this life nearly a century later.

Soon it's time to rejoin the main trail because it's already past noon, and there are many miles to cover. As Thomas Divide Trail climbs rather steeply, I look south toward the prominent Standing Indian Mountain, soaring 5,498 feet high along the Appalachian Trail, just north of the Georgia border. In a few weeks, the mountain will see heavy foot traffic from the hordes of hikers who set out from Springer Mountain, Georgia, with the goal of reaching Maine's Mount Katahdin, twenty-one-hundred miles north of Standing Indian. If history holds, about 25 percent of the 2016 "thru hikers" will make it end to end. The rest will fall by the wayside, many before reaching the Smokies. Needless to say, completing even a big chunk of the AT is not an easy feat.

Farther up the trail, I get another distant view of the Smokies' crest, this one featuring evergreen slopes clothed in snow. Soon I reach Stone Pile Gap, which these days might be called Boulder Gap instead as two boulders sit in the gap just inside the park boundary. Across from the boulders, a sign marks the beginning of Stone Pile Gap Trail, which drops sharply off the ridge before arriving at Indian Creek in slightly less than a mile. Stone Pile Gap brings back memories of the 1980s, when Karen and I stopped here and discussed how nice it must be to live in one of the houses just outside the park boundary, in the pastoral Galbraith Creek community of Swain County. I grab a quick snack as I rest in the sun on one of the boulders and then continue on Thomas Divide Trail.

I was last on this section of Thomas Divide Trail in June 2015, when I decided to take on a hike of eighteen miles round-trip to do my Adopt-a-Campsite duty at Newton Bald backcountry campsite. I thought that distance was appropriate, as I had just retired from my job at a small college after eighteen years. On this day, however, I continue on Thomas Divide Trail only a couple of miles beyond Stone Pile Gap, before picking up Indian Creek Motor Trail. As I climb toward the junction, I encounter several spots with deep gullies, apparently from heavy rains since I was last here. I also begin to see a few lingering patches of snow on either side of the trail in places that have northern exposure.

At the expansive junction of Thomas Divide and Indian Creek Motor Trails, I decide to eat a late lunch. I land on a comfortable log to the right, where Thomas Divide has left the roadbed to become an actual footpath. It's a wonderful perch in the sun, with fine distant views to my left and right. At just under thirty-five-hundred feet, it's also the highest hiking elevation I've attained all year. After lunch, I begin a steady descent to Georges Branch, Indian Creek, and Deep Creek.

Ironically, there has never been any motoring on the short Indian Creek Motor Trail. The trail—an old roadbed—was constructed as part of an ill-conceived plan to build a motor road in the area, before the project was abandoned in the mid-1970s. Today, the steep, wet, rocky trail shows definite signs of neglect; it appears to be little-used by hikers. As I continue descending, there's a large blowdown to the right, one that has split to somewhat resemble an outsized wooden crocodile's snout. Sunkota Ridge, on the far side of Indian Creek, soon looms directly in front of me. In a few more minutes, I hear the rush of Georges Branch, hurrying past the junction of Indian Creek Motor and Deeplow Gap Trails. At the junction, the trail sign indicates it's one-tenth mile to Indian Creek (*not* Motor) Trail, but if so it's the longest 176 yards in existence. Upon arriving at the latter trail, I note a sign that much more accurately states the distance is three-tenths mile.

Almost immediately after turning left onto Indian Creek Trail, I cross a bridge where Georges Branch tumbles into Indian Creek, which sparkles in the late-winter sun. A bit farther down the trail, near boxwoods that no doubt were planted at an old homestead, the ground has been chewed up by wild boar. Old-timers called them *Rooshians* because of the belief they were brought to western North Carolina from the Ural Mountains of Russia. The walking is easy and pleasant as I continue to descend gradually toward Deep Creek. After passing the lower-elevation trailhead for Stone Pile Gap, I encounter the first of many people I'll see before I arrive back at my car—hikers, joggers, even a cyclist are among the ranks who have come out, perhaps after work or school in nearby Bryson City. At the short side trail to picturesque Indian Creek Falls, two women with small children have parked a stroller in order to walk down the steep trail to the falls.

I meet up with Deep Creek Trail, where the creek's popular tubing run begins. As always, it's fun to look at the creek and recall past tubing adventures on hot summer days. Water levels today are much higher than they were for any of my tubing trips—no surprise considering the heavy rainfall and significant snowfall of the past few months. Near the car, I stop to admire Tom Branch Falls as it spills off the ridge to join Deep Creek. I offer to take a smart-phone photo of a couple in order to complement the selfie they've just shot.

Back at the parking lot, I meet friendly local residents coming and going to enjoy Deep Creek on a beautiful February day. I drive out of the lot, but soon decide to park next to the picnic ground, so that I can regroup at the spot where Karen and I enjoyed so many outings with our young sons in the late 1980s and early 90s, before moving to Florida for a few years. I'm alone except for small groups of joggers who periodically pass by. But if I close my eyes, I can imagine two little boys on a picnic—and even a tiny firstborn whose parents brought him here on Labor Day 1987 when he was only about six weeks old. Ah, the happy longtime memories of Deep Creek.

Hike 7

An Extra-day Excursion

February 29
Trail: Ramsey Cascades
*Trailhead weather
 conditions:* 58 degrees,
 partly cloudy, breezy
Round-trip miles hiked: 8.0

Today I get to close out what always seems like the longest month—leap year or not—with a new personal adventure: a hike to Ramsey Cascades in the Greenbrier section of the park. It's billed by some as the most spectacular display of falling water in the park, and I'm looking forward to finally seeing it for myself, especially with the high water of late winter. I won't be alone in visiting it today, for I'll see at least a couple of dozen hikers coming and going even on a Monday in February. Yes, Ramsey Cascades Trail is understandably a heavily traveled route.

Park trail guides and maps formerly spelled Ramsey Cascades, and the Ramsey Prong that unrelentingly feeds it, *Ramsay.* A 1964 United States Geological Survey quadrangle I have also uses the latter spelling, as does a 1972-revised relief map for the Knoxville region. But *Ramsey* has emerged and prevailed in recent years. In any case, the prong and cascades owe their existence to headwaters with an elevation above 6,000 feet. The headwaters are on the northern slopes of Mount Guyot, at 6,621 feet the Smokies' second highest peak. Flanked by Guyot Spur and Greenbrier Pinnacle, Ramsey Prong flows essentially west before meeting the Middle Prong of the Little Pigeon River a couple of miles below Ramsey Cascades.

Driving to the Ramsey Cascades trailhead is somewhat of an adventure in itself, as it involves traveling about five miles from U.S. 321 on mostly gravel roads that follow the Little Pigeon River and then the Middle Prong, which is crossed by narrow wooden bridges. The road surfaces have some potholes and ruts along the way, but on this dry day, they are in generally good condition. Obviously legions of hikers are undeterred by them.

It's still winter on the calendar, but the day has a different feel to it upon my arrival at the trailhead in late morning and not just because of mild weather. With the vernal equinox only three weeks away, the sun is much higher in the sky than it was even during my first February hike; spring seems poised to emerge soon. Daylight saving time won't begin for another couple of weeks, but standard time nonetheless provides plenty of afternoon light on this mostly sunny day. Even in this popular area, I'm surprised to find three cars already parked near the trailhead.

Right away, a pedestrian bridge crosses the Middle Prong. Just before the bridge, I stop to admire Little Laurel Branch on my right as it tumbles toward the prong. The branch serves as a small preview of the abundant falling water I'll see as I gain more than two-thousand feet in elevation before reaching Ramsey Cascades. Most of that gain is achieved over the final 2½ miles of the four-mile trail, where the initial old roadbed gives way to a footpath that is often steep, rocky, and wet, despite being well maintained.

Soon after crossing Middle Prong, I see a large split rock, featuring a small channel of water running between the massive boulders to my left. The rocky, old road that the trail follows continues to climb fairly steadily. Its route is easy to hike as a couple of unsawed blowdowns provide no real obstacle. My mind wanders to the Super Tuesday primaries tomorrow and to the rough, personal nature of the presidential campaign to date. Sure, politics is a contact sport as the cliché in-

structs, but will we survive eight more months of what has thus far been an unreality show?

The roadbed ends at a small turnaround, where an unmaintained trail to the left leads to the site of a former fire tower atop Greenbrier Pinnacle. Ramsey Cascades Trail continues at the top of the turnaround, near where Ramsey Prong flows into the Middle Prong of the Little Pigeon River. At this point, the character of the trail changes significantly as it works toward my destination. Ramsey Cascades Trail begins in earnest here, at times giving way to the traversing of rocks, large and small.

About a half-mile above the turnaround, I hop across a bold branch. Then I descend to cross a long, high, narrow foot log above Ramsey Prong. I tread carefully, aware that one misstep likely means serious injury or worse. To my right, the wooden rail and cables beneath it are most welcome. After clearing the prong, I encounter a briefly muddy track before continuing on firmer ground. In another half-mile or so, I reach two huge yellow poplars, flanking the trail as if to announce ENTER RAMSEY FOREST with its impressive array of old-growth trees. Just up the way is the king to these two princely poplars because the third is even larger—at least seven feet in diameter. These trees and others in this area fortunately were spared the logger's ax that was so active in the Smokies in the late-nineteenth and early twentieth centuries.

Above the poplars, a rugged section of trail employs a couple of dozen rock steps, recalling Arch Rock along the Alum Cave Trail, which leads to Mount Le Conte. Soon another foot log crosses Ramsey Prong, this one a dogleg-right track that's wider than the previous one and not as high. Ironically, as the trail presses on toward its terminus at the cascades, it begins to swing away from the prong, reaching an area known as Cherry Orchard. Farther up, I start to see patches of snow on either side of the trail and even encounter a bit of ice on the trail, despite today's mild weather. At last, where a sizable unnamed branch rushes toward Ramsey Prong, the trail plays out to the right and follows rocks in the branch toward today's main attraction: Ramsey Cascades.

If not the most spectacular crashing water in the entire park, the nearly one-hundred-foot cascades must be very close to that distinction. The timing of my arrival here could not be better, as the eight visitors I saw earlier heading back to the trailhead have long since departed and the afternoon hikers have yet to arrive. Because I have the place to myself, I stretch out on the prime viewing spot, a prodigious boulder that catches a slight bit of spray from the cascades. Although there's a fairly large pack of snow lingering stubbornly to the lower left of the cascades, it's warm in the sun where I relax for lunch. Beneath me is a run of water that flows from a shallow pool at the base of the cascades into a larger pool well below me. Above the high ledge, from which Ramsey Prong spills, is a brilliant blue sky, enhancing the beauty of these environs. In reaching this backcountry nirvana, I've hiked above four thousand feet for the first time all year, an altitude confirmed by a couple of nearby red spruce. It's truly a beautiful natural theater.

After enjoying solitude here for nearly a half hour, I greet a lone hiker who has joined me on the big viewing rock. He's visiting Ramsey Cascades for the first time, too, and is likewise awed by the sight. I tell him I'm turning over the lovely scene to him to enjoy, and then embark on the two-hour hike back to the trailhead. Along the way, I see more than a dozen hikers aiming for the cascades, many of them young people who might be on an early spring break from their colleges and universities.

On my way out, the sky becomes absolutely cloudless, helping temperatures rise to the upper sixties. Could I have a better day for my first visit to the renowned Ramsey Cascades? Highly unlikely. I'm in no hurry to return to the trailhead, especially considering the plentiful remaining sunlight. At the turnaround where the roadbed begins, I'm tempted to hike at least a short distance on the overgrown trail that leads to Greenbrier Pinnacle but decide to continue on Ramsey Cascades Trail. By the time I reach my car, I've hiked eight miles round-trip—certainly not a lengthy outing, but one that did include five rather strenuous miles. I am tired, but not exhausted, and that's always a good feeling. Although I hope to return to Ramsey Cascades one day, I doubt I will be able to surpass the enjoyment of this first trip to a truly stunning spot in the Great Smokies.

Footnote: In August, a tree fell across one of Ramsey Prong's foot logs, damaging it and making it impassable. Because rock-hopping across the churning prong is not a safe option, park managers had to close Ramsey Cascades Trail during an especially busy time of the year. With the trail remaining closed for the first several months of 2017, I was fortunate indeed to sail through on February's quadrennial bonus day.

Hike 8

A Stillness in Cataloochee

March 8
Trails: Big Fork Ridge,
   Caldwell Fork, Rough
   Fork
*Trailhead weather
   conditions:* 54 degrees,
   mostly sunny, calm
Round-trip miles hiked: 9.3

From downtown Asheville, it's a drive of only an hour or so to Cataloochee Valley, at the eastern end of the park. Yet the character of the valley is such that it seems a refuge from the world, even if the reintroduction of the American elk to Cataloochee early this century exponentially increased its visitation. Few spots in the Smokies evoke as powerful a sense of place as "catalooch," with its pastoral, peaceful environs framed by towering ridges that make the valley somehow seem apart even from the rest of the park.

Not that Cataloochee Valley is any easier to reach these days by car than it's ever been—you still have to earn your visit. The ten miles from busy Interstate 40 to the valley floor at times seem like a hundred, as much of the route follows a twisting, narrow, unpaved road once known as the Cataloochee Turnpike. But the tortuous road is hardly a deterrent to the throngs of wildlife watchers who come to view elk grazing in picturesque meadows, especially during the late afternoon. On this mild Tuesday morning in March, only a few vehicles have made it into the valley, similar to the numbers on most weekdays before the return of the elk that had been extirpated from these mountains since the nineteenth century. (Biltmore Estate owner George Vanderbilt unsuccessfully attempted to establish an elk herd from Yellowstone National Park on his Pisgah forest lands around the turn of the twentieth century.)

Have we really cleared another winter, a somewhat colder and wetter one than usual after a crazily mild December? One might think so on this comfortable early-March morning in Cataloochee, ahead of afternoon temperatures pushing into the seventies. Yes, the trees are bare and the fields still mostly brown, but today's conditions are decidedly springlike. If a false spring, so be it—better false than no spring at all.

I park in the small dirt area at the far end of the road that comes into the valley, my car joining just two other vehicles near a gate and trailhead for Rough Fork Trail. But instead of heading out on that trail, I walk back fifty paces or so to the Big Fork Ridge trailhead. My plan is to hike a loop of slightly more than nine miles, one that will take me to Caldwell Fork Trail and then upstream to Rough Fork Trail. Combined these three trails make for one of the most interesting and enjoyable loop hikes in the Smokies.

After crossing Rough Fork on a short foot log, I encounter several wet and muddy places on Big Fork Ridge Trail, the result of several seeps and creek branches. To my right, there's an extensive former farming area, where elk acclimation pens were set up in 2001 when the park began a five-year experimental release program that proved successful. As I begin a steep climb on drier ground, the woods are exceptionally still and silent, except for the occasional cawing of a crow. Even on this March day, hardly a breeze is stirring. The trail climbs to a sharp switchback on Big Fork Ridge, where there's a nice view of the formidable Balsam Mountain but also of several hemlock skeletons—dead trees that no doubt are victims of the hemlock woolly adelgid. It's a sad sight, one that is all too common around Cataloochee Valley.

Soon, the trail begins descending the opposite side of Big Fork Ridge, going toward Caldwell Fork. The hiking isn't easy in places, as there is quite a bit of log and limb debris, as well as some gullies from erosion. Like most trails in Cataloochee, this path is open to horses, but navigating it by horseback would be difficult in its current condition. After the trail flattens, I reach the site of an old school before crossing the churning Caldwell Fork on a slightly bowed foot log. Consistent with much of its condition, blowdowns block Big Fork Ridge Trail just before its junction with Caldwell Fork Trail. I turn right on the latter and almost immediately reach one of my favorite lunch spots in the Smokies: an open area where Caldwell Fork and McKee Branch Trails meet. With the midday sun at my back, my chosen spot is a nice log near a couple of hitching posts. A breeze freshens as I enjoy the setting, lingering for about twenty minutes before continuing up Caldwell Fork.

Just a short distance up Caldwell Fork Trail, a steep side trail leads to the graves of Levi Shelton and Elzie Caldwell, killed by Union raider Colonel George Kirk and his band of plunderers near the end of the Civil War. As the trail climbs above Caldwell Fork, I see the gap I recently hiked through on Big Fork Ridge, and then lovely cascades in the stream below me. There's a significant rock-hopping ford of Double Gap Branch just before the next trail junction, with Hemphill Bald Trail (formerly called Double Gap Trail from here to a junction on Cataloochee Divide). To the right of the trail signpost is a waist-high cairn that perhaps has been several years in the making. From here, it's not far to the attractive Caldwell Fork backcountry campsite on the opposite side of the stream. The campsite is reached via a span of split logs and then a footbridge crossing the fork. Yes, horses are allowed here too, but hikers can find inviting tent sites away from the main trail. I press on, anticipating a rewarding short side trip just a bit farther up Caldwell Fork Trail.

After a brief climb, I reach a sign noting BIG POP-LARS on a side trail to the right. One of the giants has been lopped off, likely by lightning, but the largest poplar alone is well worth the short side trip. Some of its limbs near the crown are as large as trees themselves, and its diameter surely rivals that of any yellow poplar in the park. My thoughts soon turn to son Rob, who came here with Karen and me a few years ago during winter break from college. As I visit here, he's on the eve of an ambitious tour of several national parks in Colorado and Utah, more than fulfilling the "Find Your Park" theme the National Park Service has been promoting during its 2016 centennial.

Back on the main trail, in the shadow of a large silverbell, I spot my first woodland wildflowers of the year: two bloodroots in bloom, matching their reputation as faithful harbingers of spring. The miracle of another Appalachian spring is starting to unfold. As I near Caldwell Fork Trail's upper terminus at Rough Fork Trail, there's a large, mossy boulder field stretching down the ridge to my left. I reach the junction and hear voices before meeting two young backpackers, who are getting ready to hang a left toward the Caldwell Fork campsite. They may have the site to themselves tonight.

A milky sun prevails as a thin cloud cover has now rolled in. I negotiate several large blowdowns in working my way down the trail. I then take a left into the Big Hemlock backcountry campsite amid a maze of rhododendron. For the first time, I see a broken food cable at a backcountry site, which I will later report to the park's backcountry chief. After returning to Rough Fork Trail, it's only a half-mile or so to the Woody Place, a two-story frame house built early in the twentieth century. Near its springhouse, some daffodils are poised to bloom. I continue down the trail, crossing Rough Fork on a foot log that ends in rocky running water. Then I turn right to another log that leads me to a wide roadbed on the far side. The walking—strolling, really—is easy the rest of the way, with only one more footbridge to traverse.

Back at the car, I think again of Rob and his first trip into Cataloochee as an infant, when we took a photo near the parking area of him leaning on a small cooler. (We have another photo of his older brother, Ben, at an even younger age near the old Beech Grove School a bit down the road.) I look down the valley and spot what I think are elk grazing in the field. My conjecture is soon confirmed after I drive to another parking area next to a two-story barn. The barn is across the road from the Hiram Caldwell house, another of the structures still standing in what was once a community of about twelve hundred residents. Nearby, at least a dozen elk, including a couple of large bulls, are going about the business of grazing. The elk's total numbers in the Smokies now likely exceed 150, most of them in and around Cataloochee Valley, but there are also quite a few on Balsam Mountain and in the Oconaluftee area. Although the restoration program has been a success, a recent vote by the North Carolina Wildlife Resources Commission that would allow a future elk hunting season outside the park seems premature at best.

Driving out of Cataloochee Valley, I make what is always a highly anticipated stop at an overlook shortly before the pavement gives way to gravel at Sal Patch Gap. The overlook affords stunning views of the valley and the high ridges that wall it off from the world: Cataloochee Divide, Balsam Mountain, and Mount Sterling Ridge. Is there a finer wilderness vista in the eastern United States that's only a few steps from a parking area? Not likely. The overlook provides the punctuation to another enjoyable day in Cataloochee Valley, one of the Great Smokies' undisputed gems.

Hike 9

Winter Finale

March 19
Trails: Huskey Gap,
  Sugarland Mountain
Trailhead weather
  conditions: 62 degrees,
  mostly cloudy, calm
Round-trip miles hiked: 8.2

The impetus for today's trail excursion isn't a favorable weather forecast, as has been the case with most of my outings this year. Instead, my hike on Huskey Gap Trail is piggybacking on a volunteer training session at park headquarters at Sugarlands. Although the trailhead is about two hours from my home in Asheville, it's only 1½ miles from headquarters and on the way back home. Thus, even though today's forecast includes the possibility of a cold rain, because I'm already in the neighborhood it's as good a time as any to head out on Huskey Gap Trail, just a few steps from Newfound Gap Road. The trail also offers me one last winter hike—my ninth since New Year's Day—before the vernal equinox arrives. And I must say that nine hikes before the official start of spring isn't a bad body of work (well, fun), especially considering some prolonged stretches of rough weather in January and February.

Of course, there are some advantages to hiking in the dead of winter in the Great Smoky Mountains. In addition to long-range views unimpeded by foliage and haze, among the obvious ones is the absence of pesky insects, even if they are rarely the nuisance in the Smokies they can be in some other national parks. (Black flies in Acadia and salt-marsh mosquitoes in the Everglades come to mind.) So is the absence of large numbers of humans, if solitude is a priority. But other benefits of winter hiking in the park may be somewhat subtler. One of them is a clearer view of the topography when hiking along creeks, not just along ridges. The deep folds of the mountains are much more visible in winter, minus the Smokies' famously dense growth. Another is the increased possibility of seeing—not just hearing—species such as pileated woodpeckers and seldom-seen barred owls. Often active during the day, barred owls may occasionally be spotted when the forest lacks foliage. Thus, even a warm-weather guy like me must admit that winter hiking can have much to commend it. But now I'm glad spring is at hand.

Volunteering for Great Smoky Mountains National Park several times a year has been one of my enjoyable activities in life for the past quarter-century or so. In the early 1990s, I served as a trail patroller on the upper end of Thomas Divide Trail. Then, upon returning to North Carolina after living in Florida for three years, I signed on with the Adopt-a-Campsite program that was launched in 1997. Since then I've maintained five backcountry campsites at various times, though for the past few years I've focused solely on the Newton Bald site (#52) situated at an elevation of five thousand feet, just off Thomas Divide Trail.

The morning session at Sugarlands, organized by park backcountry personnel, deals with program updates and inevitable government acronyms in regard to campsite maintenance—JHA (job hazard analysis) and SOPs (standard operating procedures). The three-hour meeting is time well spent, serving as an excellent refresher, even for those of us who've been part of the program for many years. It also gives me good inspiration to do the first of my several cleanups of 2016 within the next couple of weeks.

After the meeting, I'm able to grab the only remaining non-handicap space available in the Quiet Walkway parking area across from Huskey Gap trailhead. The parking area is located along the heavily traveled Newfound Gap Road. I'm also fortunate that the weather, although mostly cloudy, is mild and dry as I set out on the trail. The elements change soon enough, however, starting with a few sprinkles as I make my way up the approximately two miles to Huskey Gap itself.

Because I've started hiking in the afternoon, I stop for lunch after less than a mile on the trail. I find a nice rock outcrop with a comfortable place to land. After lunch—gray day and bare trees notwithstanding—there's confirmation along the trail that another Appalachian spring is taking hold, as I see wildflowers such as cinquefoil, hepatica, and delicate spring beauties. Spring ephemerals, blooming before the hardwoods have foliage, are always a welcome sight regardless of how severe the winter has been. Farther along, there's a tangle of grapevines shortly before the trail passes through an enormous field of mossy boulders.

After the trail briefly dips and then flattens, I reach Huskey Gap and an intersection with the lengthy Sugarland Mountain Trail sooner than I had anticipated. Here I have a decision to make: veer slightly left to continue on Huskey Gap Trail to its terminus at Little River Trail, or take a hard left on Sugarland Mountain Trail and follow it for a while. As I ponder the admittedly less-than-weighty decision, three young backpackers arrive at the gap from the opposite direction. Spring breakers from Illinois Tech who've been out for a week, they ask me if I know anything about Hot Springs, North Carolina, known for its namesake hot springs as well as Appalachian Trail hospitality. I share what I know, wish the backpackers safe travels, and proceed on Sugarland Mountain Trail toward the Smokies' crest.

Heading south, the trail follows a dry, acidic ridge that in places is lined with galax. I hike for about a mile before arriving at a former backcountry campsite that, not surprisingly, has been abandoned, even if the backcountry food cables are still in place and in good condition. Finding a suitable place to pitch even a small tent here would require some imagination, with it being a boulder-strewn area at the headwaters of Medicine Branch. Its most appealing feature is a large rock overhang that could provide reliable shelter from a storm. As fate would have it, I take refuge there when a light rain soon begins to fall.

I'm now left with three options: proceed farther up the trail and risk getting even wetter; turn back toward Huskey Gap; or stay put for a while in an attempt to ride out what is becoming a cold rain. I choose the second option, but soon the rain is heavier and colder, as temps have now plummeted to the low fifties. I'm a little chilled by the time I reach Huskey Gap, but I decide nonetheless that I need to take the path not taken a short while ago, toward Little River Trail. When the rain picks up again in an otherwise pleasant cove, I quickly decide to head back to Huskey Gap for a third time. I suppose I wasn't content with getting just slightly wet on Sugarland Mountain Trail.

From Huskey Gap, I finally start back down to the trailhead along Newfound Gap Road. On the descent, I tread carefully because there are many slippery roots and rocks from the light rain that has settled in. Clouds billow in the Sugarlands Valley, a few of the rising formations resembling large smokestacks. Although hardly a bluebird day, to borrow a description from golfer Jack Nicklaus, the weather hasn't been all that bad. Still, a change of clothes at Chimneys picnic area farther up the road is definitely in order for the long drive home. At a brief stop at Newfound Gap, fast-moving clouds are zooming past, propelled by a stiff, cold wind at an elevation of five thousand feet. Dry clothes, not to mention a warm car, are most welcome on the drive back to Asheville after another worthwhile, if soggy, day on the Tennessee side of the Smokies.

Hike 10

Working toward the Divide

March 23
Trail: Noland Divide
Trailhead weather
conditions: 60 degrees,
mostly sunny, breezy
Round-trip miles hiked: 7.5

On this magnificent late-March day—yes, spring is officially here—I plan to hike part of Noland Divide Trail from its trailhead near Deep Creek, just inside the Smokies' park boundary. But I won't hike far enough on the nearly twelve-mile trail to actually reach Noland Divide. From its southern terminus, the trail instead follows Beaugard Ridge for about five miles before connecting with its namesake near the summit of Coburn Knob. Noland Divide Trail then continues to work its way mostly north until it meets Clingmans Dome Road at nearly six thousand feet in elevation—more than four thousand feet higher than my starting point for today's hike. On an out-and-back day hike, I won't come close to the Clingmans skyway, but I will climb high enough to enjoy one of the park's best vantage points for long-range views, particularly on a good visibility day. Along the way, I'll travel through different forest types, if nothing quite like the spruce-fir forest at the trail's northern end. The destination, just under four miles out, is the spectacular Lonesome Pine Overlook, just off the main trail. On a clear day, several distant mountain ranges can be seen from the lookout with the naked eye.

The last three weeks of winter have been unusually warm and dry in the Smokies' region. The Asheville airport, for example, has seen barely an inch of rain this month, and temperatures have been several degrees above average. With typical March winds, today's conditions seem ripe for wildfires. And because the lower end of Noland Divide Trail follows a mostly dry ridge, rather than moist coves, any fire that begins here today will likely grow very quickly. Fortunately, even the remarkable long-range views on today's outing do not offer evidence of any wildfires, large or small.

Karen joins me on today's hike, marking the third time this year I've had company on an excursion in the Smokies. Along the way, we'll see a total of ten day hikers: a solo hiker, a couple, and a group of seven who seem young enough to be spring breakers. All have taken on a hike that rather quickly climbs from just under eighteen hundred feet in elevation to well above four thousand feet—not an elevation change to sniff at. Noland Divide Trail is well graded, however, making the climb easier than it might be otherwise.

With the trailhead close to the park boundary, it's no surprise that soon after we set out and cross Durham Branch on a modest foot log we see a few houses to our left, not far from the trail. By late April, after the low-elevation hardwoods have full foliage, the houses probably will not be visible even from this short distance away. In a few minutes, we hear the distant whistle of a train that is likely near the Bryson City depot. (Great Smoky Mountains Railroad excursion trains have been operating out of the depot since the late 1980s.) Farther along the trail, but below the path, we see the familiar white blooms of a serviceberry or "sarvis" tree—blooms that confirm another Appalachian spring has begun to unfold.

As we make our way up the trail, there's a view of Kelly Bennett Peak, rising to an elevation of about forty-four hundred feet on the opposite side of the Lands Creek drainage, which is mostly outside the national park as it wedges between Noland Divide and Beaugard Ridge. Bennett Peak, however, is just inside the park boundary—appropriately so, as Bryson City pharmacist Kelly Bennett was one of the most forceful advocates for the creation of a park in the Smokies. His brick drugstore building, built in 1905, is still in use as an antiques store in town near the Tuckasegee River. Its vertical Bennett's Drugs sign marks the historic location on Everett Street.

Our dry-ridge hiking, passing through stands of pines and second-growth hardwoods, is broken after roughly two miles by a tributary of Juney Whank Branch. As it cascades off a rock face, the small feeder forms what looks like a miniature version of Juney Whank Falls, which is much farther down the ridge. Along with those of Indian Creek and Tom Branch, Juney Whank is part of a popular trio of falls that can be viewed on a short hike near Deep Creek. This high-elevation tributary is the last flowing water we'll see today. In its vicinity, where more moisture is available than on most of the generally bone-dry Beaugard Ridge, we see a few early-spring wildflowers in bloom: violets, chickweed, hepatica, bloodroot.

Higher up, after we stop for a water break just off-trail, a couple approaches us as they ascend the trail. The woman asks if we've hiked the path before. After I answer affirmatively, she then asks how far it is to Lonesome Pine and I guess about a half-mile. My guess proves fairly accurate, as we soon arrive just below the lookout at a narrow rocky ridge, which yields stunning views of many mountain ranges and ridges. Close up, to the west and southwest, is the lower end of Noland Divide itself as its plays out between Bryson City and

Fontana Lake. On the other side of Deep Creek, Sunkota Ridge and the loftier Thomas Divide are prominent, the latter reaching up toward the Great Smokies' crest. But on this blue-sky day with excellent visibility, the views of distant ranges prove to be the real stars, especially after I reach Lonesome Pine Overlook. I pass the couple on the way to the overlook, and the woman again asks how much farther it is, as she does a third time on my way back down. I can appreciate her anticipation.

As Karen stays back at another view spot, I work my way up and finally reach the side trail of fifty paces or so to Lonesome Pine Overlook. Alas, the 135-degree turn to the left is unmarked because the sign, if not the worn post, has vanished. But this is clearly the place where I need to leave the main trail in order to make it to today's destination.

Lonesome Pine Overlook is one of the park's most dramatic lookouts—an underrated one, in my opinion. Yes, better known ones such as Chimney Tops and Charlies Bunion (and even Charlies Bunion's neighbor The Jumpoff) are well worth the hike, but I think the views from Lonesome Pine can hold their own with any of them. The rocky outcrop at the end of the side trail yields remarkable views of several ranges on a clear day. To the south are the Alarka and Cowee Mountains. To the southwest are the Cheoahs, Snowbirds, Unicois, and Nantahalas, the latter crowned by the nearly fifty-five-hundred-foot Standing Indian Mountain. To the east and southeast, I spot the towering Balsam and Plott Balsam Ranges. Combined with the nearby ridges and the Smokies' crest, the distant ranges provide me with a top-of-the-world feeling here. The Lonesome Pine Overlook actually isn't adorned by a lone pine, though there is a copse of pines just below the outcrop. In favorable weather, the overlook is one of the many spots in the Smokies that's awfully difficult to leave.

After a few minutes, I begin the short walk back to Noland Divide Trail and take the sharp right toward the trailhead. I enjoy more breathtaking views from the knife-edge ridge as I head down the path to rejoin Karen, glad that we've hiked this trail today in fair weather with pleasant breezes rather than fierce March winds.

Hike 11

Time to Go to Work

April 4
Trail: Newton Bald
Trailhead weather conditions: 58 degrees, sunny, breezy
Round-trip miles hiked: 10.8

It's April—not to worry, I'm not going to quote T.S. Eliot—and in the Great Smoky Mountains that means spring wildflowers bursting forth in an eruption of color on the forest floor. But for me, April also means it's time for my first trip of the year up to the five-thousand-foot-elevation Newton Bald campsite, which I maintain as part of the park's Adopt-a-Campsite volunteer program. It's a small camp at a gently sloping open area along Newton Bald Trail, near its junction with Thomas Divide Trail. Although not as heavily used as many backcountry sites in the Smokies, Newton Bald campsite does receive moderate use (and sometimes abuse) from backpackers as well as from horseback riders. Thus, on most cleanup trips there's a fair amount of work to do.

Today's work destination (a.k.a. campsite #52) can be reached via various routes. My favorite—a course I never tire of—departs from the northern terminus of Thomas Divide Trail, a few miles south of Newfound Gap. It's a high-elevation trip of about 5¼ miles one-way on a fine footpath, off-limits to horse travel for nearly its entire distance. Such is not the case with Newton Bald Trail, which covers roughly the same distance but gains almost three thousand feet in elevation from its trailhead near Smokemont Campground. Unlike the upper end of Thomas Divide Trail, Newton Bald Trail can be muggy and buggy much of the year, as well as muddy in places with its rocky, wet crossings of branches and seeps. But Newton Bald Trail does provide an enjoyable route overall from a trailhead that's less than 1½ hours from my home in Asheville, and it's the trail I'm taking today. On this early April outing, I expect to see not only some long-range views with most of the deciduous trees still bare, but also quite a few wildflowers along the way. Might I also see black bear and wild boar today, as I have before on this trail?

As with my previous hike on Noland Divide, fire danger is high today with dry, breezy, and mild conditions prevailing as I park near the trailhead. Although paved parking is available at a turnout along Newfound Gap Road, just a few steps from the trailhead, as usual I park across the Oconaluftee River in a more spacious paved area away from the busy road. Later, I will be doubly glad that I did because a tractor trailer—commercial vehicle ban on Newfound Gap Road notwithstanding— roars into the turnout for a brief stop just as I'm coming off the trail. In contrast, my chosen parking space is next to a lovely little branch, cascading toward the Oconaluftee.

After crossing a persistently wet area caused by a seep near the trailhead, I find that the trail leading up to two nearby horse-trail junctions is as dry as I've ever seen it—and I've seen Newton Bald Trail quite a bit. The first junction is meaningful to me, as I have a photo and a trail entry from there from a 1992 outing with our four- and two-year-old sons on a sunny, mild February day. In the journal, I've quoted our older son, Ben, as observing, "This is a nice spot." Yes, it was and is. I can't resist closing my eyes here and imagining that somehow I've traveled back twenty-four years to the days when our two little guys were invariably full of wonder on excursions into the woods.

Proceeding up the trail beyond those two junc-

tions, I hear the rush of the Oconaluftee River as I see the lofty Hughes Ridge on the other side of the river. Where the trail briefly flattens about a mile later, I stop for a quick snack and drink. Some pesky bugs are swarming near a downed log that has been pecked into submission by woodpeckers; below it is a serviceberry tree with its creamy white blooms. From this point to a junction with Mingus Creek Trail about 3½ miles farther up, Newton Bald Trail climbs almost unrelentingly to an elevation exceeding five thousand feet—the highest elevation I've attained all year.

Slightly more than halfway up the trail, after traversing most of the rocky branch and seep crossings, I stop at a familiar small gap that provides a good place to regroup before continuing the steady push toward Newton Bald. After spotting numerous early-spring wildflowers (rue anemone most profusely), I enjoy long-range views on either side of the ridge—of the Alarka and Cowee Ranges to my south and the Smokies' crest to the north. When a lone woodpecker breaks the silence, I think to myself that with today's bright sun and leafless trees I could make a strong case for wearing sunglasses. Soon it's time to resume the arduous climb toward Newton Bald. In just a few minutes, I reach the final seep along the trail. The rest of the path is dry, partly because precipitation has been spotty over the past several weeks. Near here, on a hike with Karen on a February day in the mid-1980s, I saw my first wild boar in the Great Smokies.

After about four miles of hiking, I reach a swag that might give first-time hikers on Newton Bald Trail a sense that the climbing is basically over. But I've learned from experience that such is far from the case. Soon, the trail begins a stiff climb around the southeastern flank of Newton Bald itself, gaining more than two hundred feet in under a half-mile. The trail then turns sharply right, passing a couple of red spruce, before reaching the junction with Mingus Creek Trail, which has gained even more elevation over its roughly 5½-mile course from Mingus Mill. At this point, the lengthy Benton MacKaye and Mountains-to-Sea Trails both piggyback on Newton Bald Trail for the three-fourths mile down to the campsite; the steep climbing is finally over.

As usual, Newton Bald campsite is empty upon my arrival about 2 P.M. But a fire is still smoldering in the metal fire ring and that's a concern in these tinder-dry conditions. Typically, I would scatter ashes from the ring to different spots beyond the perimeter of the small camping area, but I decide it's too risky to do so today. Instead I douse and smother the fire.

Next, I check the nearby food cables, which are in good condition though the eyebolts embedded in the trees are being overtaken by tree growth. After hanging my daypack, I walk a steep one hundred paces or so down to the site's water source, a fine spring that I've never seen run dry. I clear debris that has collected, my hands instantly chilled by the icy water emerging from the ground at an elevation of nearly five thousand feet. Then it's back to the camping area, where I remove charred limbs and logs from around the fire ring before collecting some especially unpleasant trash; I won't elaborate. Finally, I walk up a nearby knob to a satellite campsite and find that no one has rebuilt a rock fire ring that often is much too large. Although my work is now done, I'm frustrated that I wasn't able to scatter ashes

from the nearly full metal fire ring in the primary camping area. That task will have to wait until my next trip to #52.

I finish the rest of my lunch after retrieving it from the food cable and enjoy resting in the warm sun. Soon the breezes freshen across the often-windblown site, and suddenly it feels like late winter again. I decide to start back toward the trailhead, looking forward to a much easier return on the descent of nearly three thousand feet in elevation. There's a fine view of the mighty Plott Balsam Range just past the junction with Mingus Creek Trail, one of many good vistas on the way down. I stop again at the small gap about halfway down and once again the wind stiffens, bringing a chill with it. Soon I proceed toward the trailhead, which I reach without having seen another mortal soul on the entire hike. The nearly eleven-mile excursion today defines solitude. And no, I didn't see bear or boar—or any other wildlife for that matter.

Back at the car I decide to walk the short distance up to the church identified by a first sign as Smokemont Baptist Church and then by a second as Lufty Baptist Church, rebuilt in 1912. The beautiful little church in its lovely setting was horrifically violated in 2015 when the body of a man stabbed multiple times was left inside. Today, the church is as it should be: a place of peace in the afternoon sun.

Hike 12

The Trillium Trail

April 16
Trails: Kanati Fork, Thomas
 Divide
*Trailhead weather
 conditions:* 70 degrees,
 sunny, light breeze
Round-trip miles hiked: 8.0

With mild, dry (perhaps too dry) conditions forecast to prevail in the Great Smokies for the next several days, I decide that I need to take full advantage of the favorable weather. Although I continue to do day hikes rather than backpacking trips, the time seems ripe to establish Smokemont Campground, along Newfound Gap Road, as a base for three days of hiking nearby trails. Thus, on a Saturday morning, I set out for the campground, hoping to claim a good site after some of the Friday-night campers depart.

Sure enough, with the campground's RV and upper loops closed until May, Smokemont filled Friday evening, according to the friendly park employee in the campground office. But by late morning, several sites open up and I am fortunate to find that my favorite site in the lower loops—an attractive one with good privacy—is there for the taking. I pull in, pay the senior pass fee (half-price) for two nights, and make camp with a cozy one-person backpacking tent. Son Rob borrowed my larger tent for his recent ten-day blitz of seven national parks in Colorado and Utah, so I will need to sleep in the seldom-used smaller tent. Fortunately, it proves satisfactory in dry weather.

My choice of hikes today is Kanati Fork Trail, just a few miles up Newfound Gap Road from Smokemont. The short, but steep, trail gains more than two thousand feet in elevation before ending at Thomas Divide Trail. Kanati Fork Trail is an especially inviting path during the latter half of April, as its lower section has one of the most stunning displays of trilliums anywhere in the park—and perhaps beyond. Not surprisingly, the lower part is a popular trip during the Smokies' annual Spring Wildflower Pilgrimage, which will occur several days after my own Kanati pilgrimage. Today's hike also will push me past one hundred miles of hiking in the Smokies for the year.

Although it's predictably busy on Newfound Gap Road on a gorgeous spring day, I spot only three cars in the parking area for Kanati Fork (and a short Quiet Walkway stroll) upon my early-afternoon arrival there. Later, I'll learn that two of them apparently belong to solo hikers, including a young man heading back down the trail carrying an expensive camera. Yes, this is prime time to photograph spring wildflowers adorning the forest floor.

The trail wastes no time in climbing sharply from the trailhead, located just a few steps from the road. Although Kanati Fork itself isn't hard by the trail, in mid-April the fork can be seen—not just heard—to my left. That likely will change around the end of the month, when dense foliage and undergrowth will predominate. Today the forest is mostly still and open with abundant sunlight streaming through the trees. As I work my way up the trail, I see an expansive carpet of trilliums between the trail and the fork. This is followed along the trail by slope after slope of large-flowered and painted trilliums, particularly near the seeps and branches that feed Kanati Fork. It's truly a widespread and impressive display until the trail begins to climb above the moist coves it traverses. The miracle of spring in the Smokies is gaining momentum.

I finally stop to rest on a mossy rock, soon after passing a large poplar along the trail. On the ascent I enjoy fine views of the muscular Balsam and Plott Balsam Ranges. The path becomes quite narrow in places, no more than a couple of feet wide; Kanati Fork Trail is off-limits to horses for good reason. At last, after a few much-needed switchbacks ease the steep climb, the trail reaches its terminus at a junction with Thomas Divide Trail. It's been a strenuous journey to the divide, even with just a light daypack to worry about.

At just under five thousand feet in elevation, this trail junction is perhaps my favorite in all the Smokies. (I concede that my feelings about it might be different were I to visit in the dead of winter.) It's broad, flat, and peaceful unless a stiff breeze is blowing across the gap. A scattering of red spruce confirms that it's a high-elevation spot, though mostly hardwoods are found here. In addition to the trail signs, there's one other man-made fixture nearby: a rusty boar trap. When I was last up here in the fall of 2015, a wild boar was indeed poking around the trap even though it wasn't baited, and the trap had been tripped anyway. Once the hairy creature heard or saw me, it predictably snorted and ran off. Fine by me, for I would not wish to tangle with one of those ornery, tusk-equipped guys.

Although there's plenty of daylight left on this sunny April day, I could make a case for heading back to the trailhead and on to my Smokemont campsite to prepare supper and to collect a bit more downed wood for a campfire that will be welcome after sunset. But I decide that I need to hike at least a short distance on the sublime Thomas Divide Trail. I choose to walk north, toward Newfound Gap, with the expectation of seeing quite a few wildflowers in that direction on a most pleasant footpath. I'm not disappointed; on either side of a small knob named Turkey Flyup (where I've never seen a turkey flying, running, or walking) it looks as if a blizzard of spring beauties has fallen from the sky to the forest floor. There's also the typically fine view of Newfound Gap itself through the trees this time of year, the downside being the sounds of Newfound Gap Road traffic—especially from motorcycles. The mile or so I walk from the trail junction before turning around proves highly rewarding nonetheless, despite some unexpected discomfort in my right knee for one of the few times since arthroscopic surgery twenty-five years ago.

When I stop to rest after hiking back to the favored junction, it's perfectly quiet until a breeze kicks up. I savor this spot while sitting on an old log that's been on the ground for some time, hoping that my knee won't give me much trouble on the steep return to the trailhead. Fortunately it doesn't, and I'm able to enjoy the trilliums and other wildflowers again as well as some excellent views of the Balsams, Plott Balsams, and nearby ridges on the other side of Newfound Gap Road. The approximately three-mile return from the junction to the car takes barely an hour, as it's downhill all the way. Unlike my previous excursions this year, I won't be driving 1½ hours or more back to the house. Instead, I'll have a ten-minute drive back to my campsite at Smokemont. It's going to be a chilly night, but there's no chance of getting rained on, and with my small tent that's a big plus. A camp dinner of steak, baked potatoes, and green beans is going to taste awfully good.

Hike 13

A Smokies Rite of Spring

For nearly a decade, beginning in the mid-1980s, hiking Kephart Prong Trail was a rite of spring for me. True, there are more spectacular places in the Great Smokies, nearby Charlies Bunion being one of them. For that matter, so is the prong's place-name cousin, the 6,217-foot-high Mount Kephart. And no doubt there are areas in the park with greater botanical diversity. Yet in my mind, Kephart Prong embodies the essence of the Smokies, especially during spring's miraculous reawakening of the earth.

The stream's name likely has something to do with this perception. The prong is named for author and outdoorsman Horace Kephart, who sought refuge in the Smokies—in part of what he famously called the "back of beyond"—early in the twentieth century. He later wrote the enduring work *Our Southern Highlanders*, which has sometimes been grossly distorted by those who disagreed with (or took offense at) his depictions of the people he lived among. Later still, Kephart became a leading proponent of a national park in the Smokies, though he did not live to see the park's establishment in 1934.

A rich human history along the trail may be another reason. Near the trailhead, not far from where Kephart Prong joins forces with Beech Flats Prong to form the Oconaluftee River, is the site of an old Civilian Conservation Corps (CCC) camp. During World War II, after the

CCC departed, the camp housed conscientious objectors. A bit farther upstream are the remains of a fish hatchery that was operated by the Works Progress Administration in the 1930s. And at trail's end, where the Kephart backcountry trail shelter now stands in a beautiful hardwood cove, Champion Fibre Company once operated a logging camp. You can still see evidence of the narrow-gauge logging railroad that ran along the prong to the head of the cove. And perhaps, if you listen closely enough, you can hear voices, too.

But aside from the trail shelter, Kephart Prong's attractions today are essentially natural, and none more apparent than in late April when there's a stunning display of wildflowers that announce another Appalachian spring. Seeing such stalwarts of spring as the large-flowered trillium can brighten the darkest of spirits, especially after a cold, gray winter in the mountains. Little wonder that the relatively short trail, accessible as it is, ranks as a favorite of many.

Today, however, Kephart Prong Trail is just the first leg of a strenuous hike into the high mountains, reaching all the way to the Appalachian Trail (AT) and the highest elevations I've attained all year. Although there's an elevation gain of about nine hundred feet on the two miles of Kephart Prong Trail, that's only a start en route to a total gain of nearly three thousand feet. The rewards of today's ambitious hike will be hard earned.

Visible a few minutes from the trailhead, in addition to the remains of a stone structure marking the former CCC camp, are chimney ruins and an old water fountain to the right of the trail. But farther up the trail, there's a structure that has been constructed since my last visit here in the late 1990s: a footbridge, sturdily built of two-by-fours. It replaced the narrow foot log that formerly led hikers across the first of four Kephart Prong crossings.

After the bridge, the trail follows a broken macad-am surface for a while. As temperatures rise rapidly, I notice a boulder that serves as host to several trilliums in bloom on this mild spring day. I'm then startled by a low-flying hawk as he flies hurriedly, just a few feet above me, in the opposite direction. Soon there's another stream crossing, and as I approach it, a backpacker on the opposite side calls out to me.

"Hey, is there a way around this?" he bellows. He has missed the sign for the foot log, and thus reached the water's edge and a sizable pool.

"Yes, there's a foot log farther up," I advise.

After he makes it across Kephart Prong on the foot log, he asks, "How much farther to the road?" He apparently is completing a one-way trip that will end at the Kephart Prong parking area along Newfound Gap Road. I guess that it's likely no more than a mile, and he quickly makes tracks down the trail.

Continuing up the trail, I occasionally see tributaries of the prong, spilling off the ridge. I meet two more backpackers, then greet a group of seven also headed toward the road. Apparently it's been a busy Saturday night at Kephart shelter. The trail briefly becomes a jumble of rocks just before the fourth and final crossing of the prong. As I near the shelter, a number of bluets in bloom join the profusion of trilliums. After a rather steep ascent toward trail's end, I arrive at the shelter—empty near the noon hour. It's peaceful in the cove, with nothing stirring, as I spot two large evergreens on a high ridge to the west, amid the hardwoods that remain bare in mid-April.

I've camped at park shelters at Tricorner Knob and Laurel Gap with mostly considerate neighbors, but I confess that I much prefer sleeping in my own tent. In recent years, shelters in the Smokies—most of which are situated along the Appalachian Trail—have been renovated, which has made them a bit more inviting. Although I find the Kephart shelter to be reasonably clean inside, such is not the case outside, as a few back-packers have left toilet paper scattered about on the ground. Ugh.

Soon it's time to face the inevitable: a steep climb on Grassy Branch Trail to Dry Sluice Gap Trail, which will take me to the Appalachian Trail near Charlies Bunion. Grassy Branch Trail gains about eighteen hundred feet in elevation in about 2¾ miles before its terminus high on Richland Mountain, and I would not dispute even a foot of that gain. The first part of the trail is a bit decep-tive, as what appears to be a trail relocation has routed the path on a wide trail with an easy grade. That chang-es soon enough, where a narrower trail begins to climb sharply before a rock-hop crossing of Grassy Branch. Soon a few non-native Norway spruce appear to the left of the trail, perhaps pre-park plantings by Champion Fibre Company. There also are fine views looking south from the path. Within a mile of the trail's terminus, af-ter a final switchback, acres and acres of spring beau-ties can be seen above and below the trail as it courses through a moist, open cove.

None too soon, I reach a junction with Dry Sluice Gap Trail. From here, to the left, it's about 1¼ miles to the Appalachian Trail, the final half-mile or so heading downhill. From the high point on Dry Sluice Gap Trail, where there are a couple of healthy Fraser firs not yet wiped out by the balsam woolly adelgid, I spot Icewater Spring shelter on the slopes of Mount Kephart, along with an impressive view of Mount Le Conte. As I reach the AT, I briefly encounter three "thru-hikers," one of whom reports that "things are going great" a couple of hundred miles into their epic twenty-two-hundred-mile journey from Georgia to Maine. I head south on the AT, toward Charlies Bunion, while they continue north to-ward Mount Katadin.

Not many landmarks are named for an inflamma-tion on a toe joint, but such is the case with Charlies Bunion, named by Horace Kephart. (The Charlie so "honored" was a hiking buddy, Charlie Connor.) I ap-proach the dramatic rocky outcrop from the lesser-used northern side, where a bracing breeze is whipping across the somewhat precarious path. Soon, I reach the open crags, and predictably a crowd—one of young hikers mostly—has gathered on this Sunday afternoon. A dar-ing young woman strikes a one-legged yoga pose for a picture on a rocky perch above, prompting me to think a 911 call may be a possibility. But fortunately, she re-mains upright while I make my way around the Bunion to another side trail that takes hikers around the back-side to an even higher point. I find a safe spot where I can eat a late lunch and enjoy the view especially of Mount Le Conte. Its soaring profile and prominence re-semble that of Washington state's Mount Rainier—mi-nus the snow and the much higher elevation. The young hikers are getting a bit rowdy and that's OK, but when one lights up a cigarette that sends smoke my way, I de-cide it's time to depart. At the side trail's junction with the AT, I see the remains of a small fire that a hiker built, clearly in violation of park regulations.

A few minutes into the return trip, an Appalachian Trail Ridgerunner (basically a steward of the trail who assists hikers as needed) greets me just before I hang a right on Dry Sluice Gap Trail. She asks if I'm out for just the day, as seems obvious with my small pack. In turn, I ask her where she's been (Tricorner Knob) and how much longer she'll be out on her current trip. "One more night," she replies, "and then I get to go to my truck."

Shortly after departing the AT, I see huge clouds of smoke billowing in the distance—much too large for a brush fire. I'm guessing that the fire is burning outside the park on the Cherokee Indian Reservation. Sure enough, I learn later that the fire scorched about two hundred acres near downtown Cherokee, forcing closure of a main road before it was fully contained. Fortunately, the fire did no harm to humans or property. It isn't the only fire on the reservation and elsewhere in the mountains in April, as a rainfall deficit continues to worsen. But campfires create the only visible smoke when I settle in later for another clear, cold night at Smokemont Campground. Rain chances? They remain at zero.

Hike 14

Chasteen and Its Cascade

April 18
Trails: Bradley Fork,
    Chasteen Creek
*Trailhead weather
    conditions:* 51 degrees,
    sunny, calm
Round-trip miles hiked: 7.0

This morning, after another chilly night in my small tent, I break camp at Smokemont. As I do, my mind wanders to the first time I camped at Smokemont in the spring, with son Ben. The year must have been 1993, as he was nearing the end of kindergarten a couple of months before his sixth birthday. I recall reluctantly delaying our departure from our home in nearby Webster, North Carolina, until Saturday afternoon, because he had been invited to a classmate's birthday party that day. Since young Ben didn't seem to know the birthday boy very well, I thought that it might be OK for him to miss the party, before I thought better of his skipping it. Later, when I went to pick him up from the boy's house at the appointed time, I learned that Ben was the only invited friend to show up—a circumstance that fully validated delaying our camping trip. How demoralizing it would have been to plan a birthday party that no one attended.

All that was a long time ago, and I'm not quite sure why it has entered my mind on this cool, dewy morning except perhaps to underscore the fact that sometimes the woods can wait. I prepare and eat a big pot of oatmeal and raisins, then make a sandwich for a final day of hiking on my three-day exploration of trails near Newfound Gap Road. This hike is on extremely familiar terrain, as I'll walk to two nearby backcountry campsites that I maintained for several years. It's also one of my shorter hikes of the year, since even the farther campsite is only about 3½ miles from the frontcountry Smokemont Campground.

As I walk through the campground's upper loop—closed until the season starts to really heat up in May—the only sign of life I see is a wild turkey poking around. The solitude prevailing here today will change soon enough during the Smokemont reservation period, particularly from about mid-June to mid-August when the entire 142-site campground will routinely fill with campers. Today, though, it's almost eerily quiet as I walk away from the campground's lower section, which stays open year-round. After a few minutes, I reach the gate marking the beginning of Bradley Fork Trail, where I hiked in January en route to Cabin Flats Trail several miles upstream. On this excursion, however, I turn right on Chasteen Creek Trail after barely more than a mile on the old roadbed forming Bradley Fork Trail. Chasteen Creek is the largest tributary of the beautiful Bradley Fork, which flows mostly south from its source near the Smokies' crest.

At the junction of Bradley Fork and Chasteen Creek Trails, there's an unusual sight even for the not-so-remote backcountry: a parked National Park Service truck and horse trailer. (Chasteen Creek Cascade, just over a half-mile from the junction, has long been a popular destination for horseback riders.) Soon after picking up Chasteen Creek Trail, I veer off-trail to the right, into the Lower Chasteen backcountry campsite, one of the easiest to reach in the entire park. Two campers are departing just as I arrive, leaving me alone to have a snack at the site's most wide-open camping area. Near a metal fire ring, I sit on a log in the shade, as the sun has become rather intense for a mid-April day.

Back on Chasteen Creek Trail after exiting the campsite, I cross a sturdy bridge over the creek and continue toward the cascade, which I reach in about ten minutes. There's a short side trail to the left that leads to a popular spot to view the lovely falling water. A familiar hitching post is still here, as is a mounting platform that has been added since I last hiked to this spot. Although the side trail offers a nice place for close-up viewing of the cascade, I actually prefer a vantage point a bit farther up the main trail, where I can look down at the entire run. Later, above this higher point I see a sad sight: a massive dead hemlock tree next to the trail that was alive, if not healthy, the last time I passed it. The hemlock woolly adelgid has clearly exacted a stiff toll in the Smokies and elsewhere. From this area to Upper Chasteen campsite—another 1¾ miles up the main trail—there's a nice bonus for hikers: very little horse poop on the path to worry about.

As I near Upper Chasteen, high above the creek, a piece of Chasteen Creek Trail has been eaten by a mudslide. But fortunately there's still enough trail to allow safe negotiation of the area. I continue climbing toward the campsite, basically following a profusion of trilliums—my favorite spring wildflower—all the way to Upper Chasteen, or campsite #48.

Hunting is illegal in Great Smoky Mountains National Park. So are dogs—not just hunting dogs—in the Smokies' backcountry. (Leashed dogs *are* allowed on two short trails, Gatlinburg and Oconaluftee River, near busy visitor centers.) Over the past few years, however, I've seen at least a half-dozen dogs out on other trails as more and more people seem willing to flout the regulations so that good old Fido can come along for the fun. Before that, the only dogs I had seen in the backcountry were the couple of occasions when coonhounds apparently had run up and over Hughes Ridge from the Qualla Boundary to the Upper Chasteen backcountry campsite where I was camping. Each time, I used makeshift leashes to lead the dogs out of the backcountry to the Smokemont ranger station. Not that I have anything against dogs, or at least not most of them. One of my most wrenching moments in life was having to say goodbye to our fourteen-year-old Lab mix several years ago. But I fully understand and support the ban on dogs and other pets in the Smokies' backcountry, where there is plentiful wildlife but no legal hunting. Unlike national forests, the park is supposed to be a refuge for wildlife.

But back to Upper Chasteen campsite. I don't recall exactly when (probably around 2010) I gave up maintaining the backcountry site that's pleasant even if lacking in flat tent sites. I had many memorable experiences here on both day and overnight trips, including two visits when, coincidentally, thunderstorms rolled in almost precisely at high noon and produced lightning strikes that I think came as close to nailing me as any I've ever experienced anywhere. Maybe lightning does strike twice—at least near here.

As for the condition of the camp on this visit, I must say I'm disappointed in it. Someone has removed a no-camping sign I posted several years ago on a tree leading down to an illegal camping spot right by the stream. Not only is a tent pitched there (no one is home), but also a massive rock fire ring has been built nearby. Large as that ring is, it's smaller than another one some distance from the stream. Both are considerably larger than the recommended maximum diameter of two feet. Although there's not a great deal of trash around the campsite, overall the site looks as if it hasn't gotten a lot of attention in recent years. On the positive side, most of the large hemlocks at Upper Chasteen seem healthy—for now.

After lunch on a log next to a gently sloping area where son Rob and I last camped at Upper Chasteen, I start back down the trail toward Smokemont. It's a relatively quick trip out as the trail descends steadily between the lofty Hughes and Mine Ridges. In about seventy-five minutes I reach my car, now at a day-use parking area rather than the two-night campsite. I've had an enjoyable three days out, but now it's time to head home for creature comforts: a hot shower and a warm bed. Even if I'm not able to return to the Smokies till early May, I've put four April hikes in the books, and that's not a bad count for an especially appealing month in the Great Smoky Mountains.

Hike 15

Breaking a Dry Spell

May 9
Trails: Snake Den Ridge,
  Maddron Bald,
  Appalachian, Low Gap
  (Tennessee)
*Trailhead weather
  conditions:* 64 degrees,
  overcast, calm
Round-trip miles hiked: 13.5

As with the recent weather for the most part, I've had something of a Smokies dry spell since my three-day hiking adventure in mid-April. But that changes today in dramatic fashion, with a hike on Snake Den Ridge Trail. It's one of the more formidable footpaths in the entire park, gaining about thirty-five-hundred feet in elevation in 5⅓ miles from its trailhead at Cosby Campground to the terminus at approximately fifty-eight-hundred feet on the Appalachian Trail. Snake Den Ridge Trail doesn't have the most inviting of names, but it does promise to take me through varied forests and ecosystems on a long, hard slog in the general direction of Mount Guyot. At 6,621 feet in elevation, Mount Guyot is the second highest peak in the Smokies, behind only Clingmans Dome. If my legs and feet hold up, I'm entertaining the notion of a thirteen-mile loop, taking a left at the AT junction to head north and then another left on Low Gap Trail in order to return to Cosby. This is an ambitious route, to be sure, but one that should be well worth it on a pleasant mid-spring day.

Somehow it doesn't seem as if it's been more than four months since that early January day when I last set out on a hike from Cosby Campground. Ironically, that day—only a couple of weeks past the winter solstice—was much brighter than today, which is cloudy and gray upon my arrival in late morning. I drive through a deep, dark forest on the two-mile approach from the park entrance to the hiker parking area at Cosby Picnic Area. On the other hand, I won't find a crusty trail or patches of snow today, as I did on my January visit when the temperature was right at freezing upon my arrival.

Finding the trailhead for Snake Den Ridge Trail is a bit of an adventure itself, since it's not near the hiker parking area. As a sign instructs, it's located near campsite #51 in Cosby Campground, in Loop B. After parking, I walk up the road toward the loop and turn right toward that campsite. Because Loop B is still closed for the season, I take what I think is a shortcut through some other sites and finally find the trail—a gated old roadbed initially—to the right of campsite #51. I'm now ready to begin the hike in earnest.

After climbing about one-third mile from the trailhead, I spot an Eastern Cottontail munching on some greenery to the right of a junction with the Cosby horse trail. Predictably, the rabbit scampers on as I turn in its direction on Snake Den Ridge Trail. Another one-third mile or so farther up the main trail, there's a small cemetery on the right, just off the path. In contrast to the markers of several people—most of them Williamsons—who died in the early 1900s, a large rock identifies the departed Ella V. Costner as having lived from 1894 to 1982. The inscription notes that she was a United States Army Reserve nurse, World War II POW, and Poet Laureate of the Smokies, an honor formally bestowed by her home-state legislature.

Soon the old road ends at a turnaround. To the right, a side trail of just a few steps leads to a nice view of Rock Creek below. Fewer than two hundred yards up the main trail, a long foot log crosses the creek. After the crossing, amid some large hardwoods, a tangle of blowdowns has been sawed in order to clear the trail for easy passage through the area. I meet two backpackers heading down the trail, the only two people I see today not traveling the Appalachian Trail.

In less than a mile, the trail crosses Inadu Creek on rocks instead of a foot log. (*Inadu* is said to be Cherokee for "snake," consistent with the trail name.) Although the crossing isn't especially difficult today, it likely would pose a challenge if the creek were swollen.

The trail grade stiffens beyond Inadu Creek. Soon, I reach a pine/oak forest and a bone-dry stretch of trail with no creek within sight or sound. At a bend in the trail are impressive views of the Stone and English mountain masses rising up from the Tennessee foothills. I see some painted trilliums as I walk through a moister area, graced by red spruce but also by a number of hemlock skeletons that have succumbed to the pervasive adelgid. The trail traverses a small, grassy glade before I begin the rocky, wet final ascent to a junction with Maddron Bald Trail—another friend from my winter travels, as farther down it led me to the sublime Albright Grove Loop Trail. I turn left to continue on Snake Den Ridge Trail and for most of the remaining three-fourths mile or so to the Appalachian Trail I'm treated to blooming spring beauties and stately red spruce flanking the path. I'll be flirting with six thousand feet of elevation when I finally reach the AT in the shadow of Inadu Knob. (Yes, that Cherokee word again.) Early in 1984, an F-4 Phantom II fighter jet crashed near the summit of the 5,940-foot knob, killing the two United States Air Force crewmen aboard.

It's now just past two o'clock and time for a late lunch on a wrinkled rock outcrop at the AT junction. With the lofty elevation, it's noticeably cooler here, especially when a breeze kicks up. After a bite, I decide to head north on the AT, toward Camel and Low Gaps, as my knees and feet seem to be doing fine despite the arduous climb. Soon, at brief openings in the thick vegetation, I enjoy wow-inducing views of lofty Balsam Mountain and then of soaring Mount Sterling Ridge. Before reaching Camel Gap, I come to the first point in thirty miles where the mighty AT drops below five thousand feet in elevation. After briefly topping five thousand feet again, while skirting the summit of Cosby Knob, the AT dips sharply to about two thousand feet before exiting the park at Davenport Gap.

During my 4¾ miles on the AT today I don't encounter any thru-hikers headed toward Maine. But that's no real surprise, as nearly all the hikers aiming for Mount Katadin from Georgia's Springer Mountain have cleared the Smokies by now. Soon, however, I do see a couple of backpackers heading south on the AT toward Snake Den Ridge Trail, planning an overnight at Otter Creek Campsite along that trail. After the lead hiker warns me of some very muddy spots ahead, he tells me they have walked up Low Gap Trail from Lower Walnut Bottom backcountry campsite on the North Carolina side and their "knees are shot." Just on the other side of Camel Gap, I meet a young man and woman also headed for Otter Creek after hiking up Low Gap Trail, following an overnight at Big Creek Campground. After noting she's also no fan of Low Gap Trail, the winsome woman asks me how close they are to Camel Gap, and I tell her it's no more than two hundred yards or so. Camel, by the way, is likely a broken pronunciation of Campbell as it's highly unlikely a camel has ever laid toe anywhere near these parts.

As I climb toward Cosby Knob, I get a glimpse of what appears to be a red squirrel—a.k.a. mountain boomer—scurrying up a spruce tree. Sure enough,

when I reach the base of the tree, the boomer begins a loud, rapid-fire scolding, unmistakably that of the red squirrel, which is common in warmer months at high elevations in the southern Appalachians. Farther along, as I work my way around Cosby Knob, the trail is lined by a short stretch of mountain oat grass. I see a couple of serviceberry trees in bloom, a good six weeks later than when the white "sarvis" blossoms pop out at lower elevations. Soon, I spot Cosby Knob trail shelter on my right below the trail, but I decide not to visit it after smelling wood smoke and hearing voices—the campers may favor privacy.

It's mostly a rocky, wet descent from the shelter area to Low Gap and its much lower elevation of less than forty-three hundred feet. As I rest on a rock, two young women, unencumbered by even a daypack, reach the gap and quickly turn right, likely headed for the Mount Cammerer Fire Tower, just off the Appalachian Trail. Although they don't stop to talk, I'm guessing they are camping at Lower Walnut Bottom rather than hiking a long loop without packs.

I begin an even steeper descent of nearly two thousand feet toward Cosby on the Tennessee version of Low Gap Trail, not to be confused with Low Gap Trail on the North Carolina side that descends to Big Creek. A few minutes later, I see a black rat snake slithering slowly across the trail as if he owns it—maybe he does. No, I didn't spot any snakes on the somewhat ominously named Snake Den Ridge Trail, but now I've seen a four-footer on Low Gap Trail. That's OK, though, especially since this non-venomous one has no interest in me. Now that's my kind of snake: non-venomous, non-threatening.

Hike 16

Mingus Creek Trail, End to End

May 22
Trails: Mingus Creek,
   Newton Bald
*Trailhead weather
   conditions:* 62 degrees,
   mostly sunny, breezy
Round-trip miles hiked: 12.8

I began my year of hiking on New Year's Day with a short hike up Mingus Creek, veering right after about a mile onto a side trail to the humble, though beautifully situated, Mingus Cemetery. Today's route from the same parking area off Newfound Gap Road is much longer than the previous one, as I plan to hike the entire Mingus Creek Trail to Newton Bald Trail and then continue on the latter to Newton Bald backcountry campsite. Instead of about 4½ miles round-trip, I'll ring up about thirteen and gain three thousand feet in elevation in the process. Clearly, it's going to be a second consecutive strenuous outing in the Smokies' backcountry. In addition to the arduous hike, I plan to clean up Newton Bald campsite for the second time this year as part of my ongoing Adopt-a-Campsite volunteer work.

Not surprisingly, today's conditions contrast with those on New Year's Day, when it was cold and cloudy. It's a breezy, blue-sky day, with temperatures headed toward seventy, as I depart from Mingus Mill parking lot. (And, yes, the gristmill is operating today.) Of course, the weather will be considerably cooler at my destination where the elevation is about five thousand feet, though still not like the clammy mid-forties on that January outing. And once I reach Mingus Ridge after roughly three miles, I should see a fine display of mountain laurel in bloom. Winter's gray and brown, broken by a few splashes of green, has long since yielded to a late-spring range of colors today.

When I arrive mid-morning at the spacious parking lot, a massive motor home is in the process of backing and turning around in order to face Newfound Gap Road; even the generous turnaround circle at the top of the lot isn't big enough for the vehicle to negotiate. But the driver accomplishes his mission without incident and I park my car in a safe spot. It's damp as I set out on the trail, but the old roadbed I follow initially is still much drier than it was in January. I see mountain laurel in bloom, perhaps a preview of what I'll enjoy on Mingus Ridge in more than an hour. Soon I reach the junction with the cemetery side trail that son Rob and I took on New Year's Day. But this time, I bear left to continue on Mingus Creek Trail and its companion path through this part of the park: North Carolina's Mountains-to-Sea Trail.

The next mile or so of trail, following Madcap Branch, is in fact a bit maddening. The few actual branch and seep crossings aren't so bad, but at several points the path gives way to wet jumbles of rocks. It's perhaps one of the sloppiest sections of trail in the park. To add to the unpleasantness, I see horse poop in a few places even though the trail is supposedly off-limits to horses; perhaps they were park-service animals at work as I saw on a previous hike on this trail. To my left, I hear a loud crack and I wonder if a black bear might be thrashing around in the undergrowth. Not the case as it turns out—just a large limb snapping. After a couple of switchbacks, the trail finally reaches dry terrain for good as it works its way toward Mingus Ridge and a junction with Deeplow Gap Trail.

A chilling wind is whipping through the small gap at an elevation well over three thousand feet, where Mingus Creek and Deeplow Gap Trails meet—enough to make me don a long-sleeve shirt after I stop for a drink and a snack. Here, I'm near not only the Adams Creek headwaters, but also the Cherokee Indian Reservation boundary. Although I'm about to enjoy a relatively level section of trail in proceeding up Mingus Creek Trail from the junction, I'm under no illusion that my climbing is anywhere near finished as I aim for Newton Bald Trail.

After I resume walking, to my left I see some stubborn clouds clinging to Thomas Divide. I barely avoid stepping on a small garter snake in the middle of the trail, and in just a few minutes there's a replay of that. The snakes are apparently looking for sun in all the right places, on a day that has begun to feel more like mid-March than late May. In turn, I find that I'm a few days early in seeing the peak of mountain laurel in bloom along the trail, although I do see a few lovely pinkish white blossoms that have opened up.

Soon, after the trail begins to get serious again about climbing, I reach a half-dozen much-appreciated switchbacks. Once I clear those, I've completed most of the elevation gain, except for one final ascent near the Newton Bald Trail junction. At the junction, I stop for lunch on a large sun-favored log before starting the short trek toward Newton Bald backcountry campsite. Unlike the lower half of Mingus Creek Trail, horses are allowed on Newton Bald Trail and it shows in the three-quarter-mile section that is rather badly chewed up.

Upon arriving at the campsite, I'm surprised to see that someone—either a park-service employee or a benevolent backpacker—has recently given the site a good swabbing. Ashes from the permanent fire ring have been removed and scattered as have any charred logs, and there's very little trash to pick up. But I'm not exactly disappointed, for it's never a bad thing to find a clean campsite. The small satellite camping area on a nearby knoll also is fine, even though it has numerous hoofprints. My only real tasks today are checking the food cables and cleaning the camp's nearby spring, which as usual has a good flow. The sole problem—a minor one—is that blowdowns have blocked the lower part of the path to the spring, requiring a steep, slippery detour. After I return to the main camping area and retrieve my small backpack from one of the food cables, I check my small hiking thermometer and see that the temperature has barely matched the campsite number: fifty-two. That's chilly for late May even at five thousand feet, especially with the wind factored in.

It's soon time to head back. As I approach the Newton Bald/Mingus Creek trail split I see a couple—the first people I've seen on the trail today—taking a breather. I learn they've also hiked up from Mingus Mill but are headed back down on Newton Bald Trail toward Smokemont, where they say they have a scooter to take them back to the mill parking area. As we broaden our conversation to the national park system, the middle-aged Tennesseans note that they've visited forty-three of our fifty-nine national parks, despite not having seen any of the eight in Alaska. In just a few weeks, they plan to notch four more in the lower forty-eight states. Suddenly I feel like a slacker.

The trip down Mingus Creek Trail goes quickly—a little too quickly at one point, because soon after reaching the Madcap Branch section I slip on a slick railroad tie but, fortunately, steady myself with my hiking pole. Just down the way, a vine that must be a hundred feet long hangs in the middle of the trail and, of course, I feel compelled to grab onto it for a short ride, age sixty-four or not.

As I near the parking area, I see a couple across the creek creating a photo op at the sluice where water goes rushing into the millrace for Mingus Mill. I arrive at the car about 4:30 P.M., just in time for me to visit the mill to watch it grinding cornmeal before its five o'clock closing. After that brief diversion across the creek, I return to the car and grab my last sandwich, which I eat just above the parking area at the site of a small slave cemetery that I've finally located after a futile attempt in January. As I relax, I wonder what stories these long departed might tell on a beautiful spring day in the Smokies.

Hike 17

Nearing Bryson Place

May 28
Trail: Deep Creek
Trailhead weather
conditions: 70 degrees,
sunny, slight breeze
Round-trip miles hiked: 11.5

Today's excursion represents a departure from previous outings this year. For one thing, it's being driven mostly by a desire on the part of Karen and me to join son Rob on the first leg of his late-breaking backpacking trip on Memorial Day weekend. With most backcountry campsites heavily booked, he was fortunate to secure the sixth and final spot available at Nettle Creek, located nearly eight miles up Deep Creek Trail. Coincidentally, I camped there in the fall of 1990, when Rob was less than a year old. I'm excited that he's camping at the site tonight, as I remember it as one of the more pleasant backcountry sites I've stayed at in the Smokies—small and remote with mostly level tent spots.

Another difference is that, unlike my trip to the Deep Creek area in February, there's no expectation of solitude on this outing. Not only is it a Saturday on a holiday weekend favored by low fuel prices, but also the weather today is basically spectacular. A popular place especially during the summer, Deep Creek will no doubt attract a large number of visitors today engaged in various activities in warm, sunny weather: camping, picnicking, hiking, tubing, and fishing. Admittedly with some trepidation, we decide to join the throng enjoying one section of the nation's most heavily visited national park.

As we drive into Bryson City late in the morning on

our way to Deep Creek, its streets are teeming with more traffic than I recall ever seeing here. Still, there are no big delays, as even the Everett Street crossing of a few Great Smoky Mountains Railroad cars takes less than a minute. But with this many vehicles in town during the holiday weekend, there's no doubt we're going to see plenty of people once we enter the park a few miles away. And yes, that expectation soon proves accurate. The spacious parking area for vehicles and horse trailers at the Noland Divide trailhead (where Rob is leaving his car) just inside the park boundary is wide open, but not so with other parking areas—those for the picnic ground, picnic shelter, and day use are overflowing. Thus we decide, after some hesitation, to park our other car in a pullout for a picnic table and walk the few hundred yards along Deep Creek Road to the trailhead for Deep Creek Trail.

Of the many beautiful streams in the Great Smoky Mountains, Deep Creek surely ranks among the prettiest. Born near Newfound Gap on the North Carolina side of the Smokies' crest, Deep Creek flows mostly straight south on its way to joining the Tuckasegee River in Bryson City. The stream's main tributaries are its Left Fork, starting near Clingmans Dome, and Indian Creek, spilling down from its source near Thomas Divide. But Deep Creek is fed by many other creeks and branches as it descends from about five thousand feet to less than two thousand feet on its lengthy run. For nearly its final mile inside the park, Deep Creek is heavily populated during the summer by people, young and not-so-young, tubing downstream, even when water levels are low. But above the tubing put-in near the mouth of Indian Creek, fly fishermen rule the waters of Deep Creek most any time of year.

Deep Creek Trail follows an old roadbed for its first couple of miles before giving way to a trail constructed in the 1930s, after the federal government took possession of most of the watershed. We start walking, along with many other people coming and going, on the gravel road above the busy turnaround for tubing drop-offs. After a few minutes, we stop to admire the eighty-foot Tom Branch Falls, spilling in a nearly straight drop from the ridge on our right. I observe that the falls have much less water than they did in February, but that's no surprise with rainfall being scarce over the past three months.

Soon, amid the tubists, fishermen, fellow hikers, and even a cyclist or two, we reach the junction with Indian Creek Trail, where we turn right for the short walk up to Indian Creek Falls—actually a cascade with considerably more water than Tom Branch Falls. Even with a lower volume than a few months ago, the falls are no less beautiful on this late-May day.

We double back to rejoin Deep Creek Trail, turning right to continue upstream. The trail is starting to become less crowded, though there are still a number of hikers who likely are hiking the Deep Creek Loop that crosses Sunkota Ridge in connecting Deep and Indian Creeks. Soon there's an opening in the vegetation that affords a fine long-range view of Deep Creek framed by that same ridge. After crossing a bridge and passing a right turn for Deep Creek Loop—where some apparently exhausted backpackers are sprawled—we arrive at the old Jenkins Place, an area where a large farm was once located. We then reach a road turnaround, where we bear right and begin hiking on a much narrower footpath that extends for about 12½ miles, all the way to Newfound Gap Road. We won't hike nearly that far today, however.

Above Jenkins Place, the trail begins climbing the first of several spurs that reach down from Sunkota

Ridge. Although these spurs increase the difficulty of the hike, in some places they also afford fine views of Deep Creek well below the trail. After a relatively short, moderate initial climb, the trail descends to a crossing of Bumgardner Branch and the first of several backcountry campsites along Deep Creek Trail.

The broad, flat Bumgardner Branch campsite, located along Deep Creek, is unusually attractive despite its heavy use. Even with a published capacity of twenty people and four horses, it often reaches that number, partly because it's only 2½ miles from the nearest parking. Today it seems well on its way to exceeding that number, official maximum or not. Immediately beyond the camp, we begin a longer, stiffer climb over the next spur, one that is highlighted by a nice, open view of a particularly beautiful stream scene: the aptly named Dancing Branch tumbling into the opposite side of Deep Creek. Farther upstream, there's another especially scenic view, this one of Noland Divide towering over a long, winding section of Deep Creek white water. We're compelled to stop and admire the stunning vista for a couple of minutes.

McCracken Branch, about 2½ miles above Bumgardner Branch, is the next backcountry campsite, and it, too, is uncommonly handsome. With a published capacity of ten (no horses), it's much smaller than the Bumgardner Branch camp. A couple of logs, near the food cables but away from the tent sites, provide an ideal spot for a late lunch. As we enjoy our sandwiches, a lone deer—the second we've seen today—pokes around the camping area, not the least bit skittish about our presence nearby.

After lunch, we depart McCracken Branch and continue upstream on Deep Creek Trail. Soon we reach the Nicks Nest Branch backcountry site, an even smaller, if less secluded, camp than McCracken Branch. Karen and I decide to climb one more spur from here before stopping shy of the prodigious Bryson Place backcountry campsite, where *Our Southern Highlanders* author Horace Kephart made his final "permanent" camp in the Smokies. We reluctantly say goodbye to Rob, who will press ahead past Bryson Place to Nettle Creek, while we backtrack toward the busy Deep Creek picnic ground.

Hiking back, we miss the good cheer of our younger son, who has reconnected with the outdoors in a big way this year. In March, after the wedding of friends in Denver, he embarked on a whirlwind tour of seven national parks in ten days in Colorado and Utah, thereby doubling the number of national parks he's visited over his twenty-six years. He will notch three more new to him—two in the West and one in the East—before the end of the National Park Service's centennial year. Now living in Raleigh, he is on his second trip to the Smokies this year, having joined me on my first outing of the year on New Year's Day. His current excursion is much more ambitious than that short day hike, for tomorrow he plans to hike Pole Road Creek Trail up to the imposing Noland Divide, so that he can enjoy some outstanding long-range vistas before returning to his car. As usual on the divide, Lonesome Pine Overlook will be the highlight.

The return hike for Karen and me is uneventful, except for an odd sight shortly past Bumgardner Branch campsite: three backpackers who, in addition to their packs, are hand-carrying full gallon jugs. One of them is even hauling a cooler. Apparently the close-in backcountry sites can attract all sorts of unusual supplies and equipment, especially on a holiday weekend. A member of the trio understandably asks me how far it is to the campsite and I reply about a half-mile. Yes, there's going to be quite a crowd tonight at Bumgardner Branch campsite, while Rob enjoys the serenity of Nettle Creek.

Hike 18

Mighty Mount Le Conte Calls

June 10
Trails: Appalachian, The Boulevard
Trailhead weather conditions: 62 degrees, sunny, light breeze
Round-trip miles hiked: 16.4

June in Great Smoky Mountains National Park is a month that begs hiking in the higher elevations. The days are long, of course, allowing for plenty of time to explore less-accessible high terrain, where temperatures are generally more comfortable than they are at lower altitudes in June. Too, the long-range views of waves and waves of verdant mountains can be jaw-dropping on a clear day. But perhaps a still bigger payoff up high is the opportunity to enjoy the showy colors of flowering shrubs: flame azalea, Catawba rhododendron, and mountain laurel. In the Smokies, the two most popular spots for doing so in mid- to late June are Andrews and Gregory Balds, each of which is relatively easy to reach on a day hike. Gregory Bald, near the southwestern corner of the park, is especially renowned for its fabulous display of blooming flame azalea, with colors ranging from creamy white to bright red. It really is quite a show, one that I plan to see as the month wears on. In the meantime, however, there's another mountain on the agenda.

Mount Le Conte, at 6,593 feet, falls 50 feet short of Clingmans Dome as the highest peak in Great Smoky Mountains National Park and 28 feet shy of runner-up

Mount Guyot. But no mountain in the Smokies is more majestic or alluring, or offers so many enticing spots and remarkable lookouts near its summit. My favorite place on Mount Le Conte, even though I've never seen one of the highly touted sunrises from its rocky outcrop, is Myrtle Point on the eastern side of the massive mountain. To the west, on the opposite side of highest-point High Top, Cliff Top yields the most spectacular sunset views. But having visited only on day trips, regrettably I've missed out on both dawn and dusk atop Mount Le Conte. One of these nights I should stay at Le Conte's trail shelter or rustic lodge; certainly that would be much easier than doing a long out-and-back day hike.

It's no accident that several trails lead to Mount Le Conte from various directions. The shortest and most dramatic is Alum Cave Trail, a mostly stiff climb that takes hikers past several fascinating geologic features. Heavily traveled most anytime it's not icy, Alum Cave Trail was closed for trail restoration Monday through Thursday for several months in 2016. Although I'm hiking on a Friday, I opt today for a longer route to Mount Le Conte that's not quite as popular: The Boulevard Trail, reached via the Appalachian Trail from Newfound Gap. I've got a full day ahead of me—a round-trip of more than sixteen miles, all of it above five thousand feet. But in my view there's no more enjoyable time to hike the demanding route than on a warm, sunny day in early June.

Newfound Gap, on the Tennessee/North Carolina state line, is almost always a busy place during daylight hours, at least when Newfound Gap Road is open from Cherokee, North Carolina, to Gatlinburg, Tennessee. It certainly was busy on September 2, 1940, when President Franklin D. Roosevelt officially dedicated the park in a ceremony more than six years after its establishment, and about two months before he was elected to an unprecedented third term. Early on this June morning, however, the large parking area still has plenty of available spaces. I pull into one at the far end of the upper level, likely away from most of the many vehicles that will come and go today.

As might be expected with such a spacious parking area, if there's a busier section on the entire twenty-two-hundred-mile Appalachian Trail than the four miles from Newfound Gap to Charlies Bunion, I'm not sure where it would be. But on this day, by getting an early start and hanging a left after 2¾ miles to pick up The Boulevard Trail, I will see dozens of people by day's end rather than hundreds. At the trailhead, before entering a dense, dark, high-elevation forest, a sign noting that it's 1,972 miles to the AT's northern terminus in Maine, as usual, makes me feel a bit wimpy. Of course, by this date most AT thru-hikers still out on the trail have passed the sign several weeks prior, after having hiked more than two hundred miles north from the Springer Mountain, Georgia, starting point.

After just a few minutes of hiking, I catch up with two older women, one of whom calls me a "long-legged hiker." I can't contest that assessment; perhaps that would be my trail name if I were a thru-hiker. Though I don't ask, I assume they're aiming for Charlies Bunion and its dramatic rocky lookout. I wish them well and continue up the trail, which does a dance between North Carolina and Tennessee, and the counties of Swain and Sevier, until it finds The Boulevard junction. On the Tennessee or northern side, the trail is predictably wetter and somewhat rockier. The North Carolina side offers some magnificent long-range views of distant mountains, in some cases partly because of dead Fraser firs, stripped of their lush growth by the balsam woolly adelgid. But soon a Tennessee section, seen through the trees, yields a fine view of today's destination and its three most prominent points: Myrtle Point, High Top, and Cliff Top. In bloom along the AT are some bluets and rhododendron, the former an early spring bloomer at lower elevations. I pass a friendly middle-aged couple, who confirm they are headed for Charlies Bunion. As I walk ahead the woman has a parting request: "Please scare the bears away; I'm terrified of them." But on this day, I will see no bears to scare even if I could, either on the AT or The Boulevard. All I spot on the trail are a few red squirrels, who are in their element in the high-elevation forest in June.

Within an hour, I arrive at The Boulevard junction, where a sign is attached to the trail post warning that Alum Cave Trail is currently closed Monday through Thursday. It's a moot point on this Friday, of course, especially since I've decided to hike out and back on The Boulevard. I turn left, and in fewer than one hundred yards, stop for a drink and snack. As I rest, three young hikers pass by on their way to Mount Le Conte. After the break, I quickly reach the Jumpoff side trail, which I recall being rough and overgrown on its half-mile route to the summit of 6,217-foot Mount Kephart and then to a precipitous lookout. With plenty of hiking and exceptional views ahead of me today, I don't even think about taking the side trail. As for The Boulevard, it's about to begin a lengthy descent of about five hundred feet to the low point on the trail. The drop is rather demoralizing, as I realize I'll be making the return climb late in the day near the end of a long hike. But, at the dip where the trail finally bottoms out, there's an impressive view into the Tennessee foothills to the right.

I press on, enjoying some Catawba rhododendron in bloom to my left as well as fine views through openings on either side of the trail. Soon, a sharp bend in the trail with good places to sit invites another rest stop. After I resume hiking, I begin one more descent, to

Alum Gap at about fifty-eight hundred feet, before the final arduous ascent up the backside of Myrtle Point begins in earnest. This climb in itself offers some terrific views, especially in an open area caused by a landslide. A narrow rock ledge, perhaps sixty feet long, offers safe passage—with the help of a sturdy hand cable—through a sizable expanse of loose rocks. I try to be extra cautious, as the views looking east from here to the Smokies' crest, Greenbrier Pinnacle, and even to distant Cold Mountain provide a spectacular distraction to achieving sure footing. The remainder of the trail up the rear flank of Myrtle Point also begs caution because much of it is rocky, wet, steep, and narrow—sometimes with little margin for error. Finally, I spot some sand myrtle in bloom, which I take as a signal that the short side trail out to Myrtle Point isn't far now. The signal proves accurate, for very shortly, The Boulevard switches back in the direction of Myrtle Point and the short side trail that leads out to the dramatic lookout.

Shortly after embarking on the side trail of one-fourth mile, I encounter two women walking back from Myrtle Point. One of them informs me that it has "lots of bugs. But it's still nice." I guess nothing in life is perfect, though I have to wonder after arriving at the point and its unsurpassed views of lush green mountains and ridges to the east, south, and west. The spot is ethereal on a warm, clear day such as today. And no, bugs aren't really much of a problem. I have the outcrop to myself after another hiker departs a couple of minutes later, and I take full advantage of the solitude for at least a half hour. I eat a late lunch during that time, joined only for a couple of minutes by a vireo poking around the rock. Below me, at fairly close range, are notable landmarks such as Peregrine Peak, Huggins Hell, and Anakeesta Ridge. But I'm more enamored of the two highest peaks in the park, Clingmans Dome to the southwest and Mount Guyot to the northeast, as well as distant ranges such as the Unicoi Mountains quite a bit farther to the southwest. Words fail—at least mine do—in describing the vistas on a clear day.

I finally decide it's time to move on after spotting and picking up a child's cap adorned with mouse ears on top and embroidered with the words CLEVELAND METROPARKS. I'm thinking it's a good candidate for the lost-and-found at LeConte Lodge, even if its owner is likely long gone from the mountain. (*Footnote:* There is some debate over whether the mountain is named for geologist Joseph LeConte or for his physicist brother, John. In any case, the brothers did spell *LeConte* as one word. Thus, the lodge spelling is correct, even if park maps spell the mountain *Le Conte*.) I rejoin The Boulevard Trail and press on to High Top, Mount Le Conte's highest point at just seven feet shy of sixty-six hundred feet; the top of a large cairn on the forested summit may actually achieve that elevation. As I descend the western slope of High Top, I stop to enjoy a close-up view of Myrtle Point before continuing to the Le Conte trail shelter, currently closed, as it often is this time of year because of aggressive bear activity. From there, it's a short walk down to LeConte Lodge, humming with overnight guests who have arrived by mid-afternoon, most of them likely via Alum Cave Trail. I stop at the office to drop off the cap, poke my head in the dining hall, draw some water from a spigot between the two buildings, and head back toward The Boulevard.

On the way back to High Top, I turn right to visit an open, grassy area just left of the side trail to Cliff Top. The expanse offers wonderful views, especially to the south. I return to The Boulevard. After passing the short trail to Myrtle Point, I begin the steep, rocky descent down the mountain. Not far past the rock-strewn slide area, I hear voices to the right of the trail, and sure enough the two women I saw early this morning are taking a break on their way to LeConte Lodge, not Charlies Bunion. One of them asks how far they are from the lodge and I guess about 1½ miles. "Well, supper isn't served until six," she cheerfully observes. With their slow-but-steady pace they should arrive in time for the highly anticipated event.

Farther along, I stop again to rest at the big bend in the trail around Anakeesta Knob; a towering dead Fraser fir stands ghostlike to my left. Later, on the lengthy ascent from the trail's low point, I stop to splash my face in the cold headwaters of Walker Camp Prong, the only water source between High Top and Newfound Gap. After meeting up again with the Appalachian Trail, I see a half-dozen backpackers within a few minutes, and wonder if their numbers ever slow on this section of the AT. Soon I hear the roar of motorcycles on Newfound Gap Road, and then see several children and parents hiking at least a short section of the mighty Appalachian Trail.

After exiting the trail, I'm compelled to climb the rock steps to the broad overlook where FDR delivered his dedication remarks nearly seventy-six years ago. After a brief stay at the top, I descend the steps to read the Rockefeller Memorial plaque, headlined by the words FOR THE PERMANENT ENJOYMENT OF THE PEOPLE. Let's hope that noble ideal remains intact for generations to come.

Hike 19

The High(est) Country

June 23
Trails: Forney Ridge,
Clingmans Dome Bypass,
Appalachian
*Trailhead weather
conditions:* 65 degrees,
mostly cloudy, breezy
Round-trip miles hiked: 6.2

Long rated by some hiking guides as easy-to-moderate, the short hike out Forney Ridge Trail to Andrews Bald was, in fact, not at all easy to walk until several years ago. Rocky, wet, eroded, heavily traveled—all these elements made the trail quite difficult to hike. Fortunately, that has changed thanks to the trail reconstruction work of park staff and volunteers, work funded by an endowment called Trails Forever. New drainage structures, steps, planks, and other elevated sections make today's short hike from the Clingmans Dome parking area to Andrews Bald considerably more pleasant. As for the destination, it remains one of the most inviting in the entire park, especially in mid- to late June, when the grassy bald's flame azalea are erupting in a profusion of color. But the views from atop Andrews Bald are impressive anytime the skies are reasonably clear.

Because it's less than two miles one-way on Forney Ridge Trail to Andrews Bald, I've decided to tack on some extra mileage to today's excursion. On the return trip, I plan to pick up the short Clingmans Dome Bypass Trail to the Appalachian Trail; head south for a short distance on the AT to Mount Buckley, the little-known but fourth-highest peak (6,580 feet elevation) in the entire park; double back on the AT to reach the Clingmans Dome summit and observation tower; and then join the hordes of people walking the paved path to and from the

Clingmans Dome parking area, itself situated at about sixty-three hundred feet in elevation. But even with the additional mileage, I'll hike just over six miles total, one of my shortest trips all year.

Karen joins me on this outing, and we are both stunned by the traffic jam we encounter on a weekday at the large Clingmans Dome parking lot. Not only is it overflowing with vehicles large and small, but also traffic through the lot has halted because the driver of a large recreational vehicle is blocking—for whatever reason—the traffic flow. Finally the RV inches forward, and soon we are fortunate to land a space that has just opened up. Even on typically busy summer days, we've never seen traffic and crowds like this at Clingmans Dome. But in just a few more minutes, we're on the Forney Ridge Trail, away from the clamor of the parking area.

The quiet and coolness of the trail, piercing the high-elevation forest, provides an almost immediate refuge. We see dozens of people hiking to and from Andrews Bald on this hot summer day in the valleys, but not so many that we feel as if we're dodging hikers all day. It's a terrific time to be up high, especially since we do not have even a drop of rain in an area that receives an average of eighty-five inches of rainfall annually. We soon stop for a bite to eat, savoring our hard-earned environs even more than our sandwiches. Farther down the trail, there's an opening in the spruce-fir forest that yields a good view of Andrews Bald. At 5,920 feet, the grassy bald is nearly 400 feet lower than the trailhead. We continue descending on Forney Ridge Trail until it reaches a junction with Forney Creek Trail, the latter stretching about 11½ miles before ending at the Lakeshore Trail near Fontana Lake.

Just past the junction, the trail finally starts to ascend. In less than a mile, it emerges from the forest to reach the open, grassy bald that got its name from a corruption of the first name of nineteenth-century cattle herder Andres Thompson. We wander through lush mountain oat grass on several short side trails in order to enjoy closer views of flame azalea in full bloom, most of them a bright orange. As for long-range views, today they are somewhat limited by typical summertime haze and clouds, but especially prominent to the southwest is the nearly mile-high High Rocks along Welch Ridge—a lofty perch Karen and I doggedly hiked to on a four-day backpacking trip thirty years ago. Also clearly visible is the sprawling, man-made Fontana Lake. Unless the weather is foul, Andrews Bald is truly a summertime garden spot in these mountains.

The origin of mountain balds remains unclear despite several theories. But what is clear is that natural succession (led most notably by tree growth) would have overtaken much of Andrews and Gregory Balds if the National Park Service had not begun managing them in 1983, so that they would remain mostly open. Strong public opposition to a 1979 park service proposal to allow natural succession to occur on all grassy balds in the Smokies prompted the park to institute a management plan for Andrews and Gregory, enabling visitors to continue to enjoy those two balds' grand views and showy flowering shrubs. In contrast, grassy balds such as Parson Bald, just south of Gregory Bald on a former section of the Appalachian Trail, have closed in dramatically since the 1980s. But on this pleasant summer day on Andrews Bald, we are enjoying the results of that ongoing management plan.

A dozen or so hikers are wandering around Andrews Bald during our stay of perhaps forty-five minutes on the bald. Except for someone's odd yell at one point, the quiet is broken only by an occasional nearby voice. Encompassing several acres, the bald is large enough to make it easy for us to feel as if we have it mostly to ourselves. On the lower part of the bald, we take turns sitting on a comfortable rock rising up from the swards of mountain oat grass. It's a wonderful perch as the warming sun pops in and out of the clouds.

On the return trip, we overtake a few groups of hikers who are struggling with the steeper sections past the Forney Creek Trail junction. Even if perhaps not in the best of shape, they deserve credit for venturing nearly two miles from their cars and the clogged parking area. They have decided to take on one of the park's most rewarding hikes, short or long.

Soon we arrive at the junction with the Clingmans Dome Bypass Trail, leading left about one-half mile to the Appalachian Trail. As Karen heads toward the parking area, I take the rocky bypass to the AT and meet several hikers coming down the bypass trail. But somewhat ironically, I don't see a single soul after I reach the AT and begin walking south to Mount Buckley and then back north to Clingmans Dome. It takes me only a few minutes to attain the summit of Mount Buckley, just 63 feet lower than Clingmans Dome's elevation of 6,643 feet—the loftiest peak in the park. For the first time this year, I hear a veery—a high-elevation bird with a distinctive song that sounds almost muzzled. Because the forest limits the views from Mount Buckley's peak, I decide to descend somewhat sharply for a few hundred feet till I reach a lovely, open area to the left. From this spot, I have exceptional views of nearby High Rocks and the more distant Gregory Bald.

I start back north toward Clingmans Dome. After again clearing the Mount Buckley summit, I have a straight-on view of the dome's observation tower until a bank of clouds obscures it. Fortunately the cloud bank has dissipated by the time I take a short side trail off the AT toward the paved path that leads to the tower. I climb the spiral ramp leading to the circular viewing platform, which allows panoramic vistas when the summit isn't bathed in clouds.

Opened in 1959 amid some controversy over its unusual design, which resembles a flying saucer that landed on a pillar, the lookout tower was chosen a couple of weeks after our visit to receive a grant of $250,000 from Partners in Preservation. The money will be used to correct foundation settlement and general deterioration of the concrete structure, stone masonry walls, and the flagstone terrace. Unfortunately, throughout most of its life the tower has yielded views marred by the sad sight of countless Fraser firs killed by the balsam woolly adelgid, likely with an assist from acid deposition. But Clingmans Dome, or Old Smoky as some still call it, endures as the crown of the Smokies, a peak nearly as high as one can get east of the Mississippi River.

Hike 20

Flame on the Mountain

June 25
Trails: Twentymile, Long Hungry Ridge, Gregory Bald, Wolf Ridge
Trailhead weather conditions: 68 degrees, sunny, calm
Round-trip miles hiked: 15.7

Just two days after my trip to Andrews Bald, I'm fortunate to visit Gregory Bald, the other grassy bald in the Great Smokies known for a stunning display of flame azalea in mid- to late June. But today's hike is a study in contrasts from the short, high-elevation path to Andrews. For one thing, the route is a long loop of more than fifteen miles, starting from the remote Twentymile section of the park. But an even more striking difference is the fact that the trailhead elevation, at about thirteen hundred feet, is five thousand feet below that of Forney Ridge Trail's starting point. With afternoon highs headed toward ninety degrees in the valleys, I'm facing a toasty, strenuous hike up to the 4,949-foot Gregory Bald. It's a day to lace the boots tightly and gear up for a long, hard push to one of the Smokies' most beautiful spots, especially in June.

After an early start from Asheville, I drive more than two hours, mostly through thick morning fog, to reach the distant trailhead. I arrive at Fontana Village Resort in slightly under two hours, but Twentymile is several winding miles on N.C. 28 beyond that. At the Lake Cheoah bridge below Fontana Dam, the road leaves Graham County to re-enter Swain County, which I departed on that same state highway more than a half hour ago. The Swain reprise is the result of the damming of the Little Tennessee River during World War II, creating Fontana Lake and flooding several Swain County communities and an old state highway. Decades later, construction of a new road the federal government had promised to build along Fontana's North Shore was halted by environmental concerns. Today the National Park Service calls the several completed miles, ending at a long tunnel, Lake View Drive; many local residents refer to it—not affectionately—as The Road to Nowhere.

But enough about Fontana, for now. I finally exit N.C. 28 to follow a broken park road that leads past the Twentymile ranger station to a small gravel parking area—yet another stark contrast to my previous hike—allowing access to Twentymile Trail. The mileage refers to the distance Cherokee Indians were forced to march in 1838, as part of the Trail of Tears removal, from a point along the Little Tennessee River to Dalton Gap at the Tennessee state line. (The Appalachian Trail passed through Dalton Gap before being rerouted after World War II to cross Fontana Dam.) Quite by coincidence, my long loop starting up Twentymile also is my twentieth hike of the year. These days, the Twentymile Trail follows an old rail grade used in the 1920s by the Kitchen Lumber Company for its extensive logging operations. The Civilian Conservation Corps upgraded it to a jeep road in the 1930s.

The formerly heavily logged forest is dark, damp, and humid as I head out just after 9 A.M.; the moderate drought in Asheville seems a world away here. Though not exactly jungle-like, the hiking conditions do seem like a steam bath for a while. To my right, many Rosebay rhododendron shrubs are blooming along Twentymile Creek. The creek is strewn with fallen trees, many of them likely toppled by a fierce storm that blew through here several years ago. In a half-mile, just above a bridge

crossing Moore Springs Branch, I reach a junction and turn right to continue on Twentymile Trail instead of Wolf Ridge Trail, which heads left up the branch. Just above the junction, a short side trail leads to fine views of Twentymile Creek Cascade.

After another 1¼ miles, I arrive at the Twentymile Creek backcountry campsite, where a young woman is breaking camp. I veer off to an annex of the site, out of her sight to give her some privacy, and have a mid-morning snack: sweet rolls that I bought at the Fontana Village convenience store along N.C. 28. We meet and talk later, after we've made the moderately steep, and somewhat drier, climb to Proctor Field Gap and an expansive trail junction. She's planning to continue on Twentymile Trail toward the Appalachian Trail and the Shuckstack fire tower, which yields remarkable views. She says that she too lives in Asheville, offering almost apologetically that she moved there from upstate New York about three years ago. I note that I'm also an outlander, from neighboring Georgia. From here, my route will be to the left or west of hers, on the Long Hungry Ridge Trail that climbs to the Gregory Bald Trail at Rich Gap. (A third trail—the Twentymile Loop Trail—also exits Proctor Field Gap.) We wish each other well as I begin the 4½-mile climb to Rich Gap.

Quickly, the walking gets rather sloppy as Long Hungry Ridge Trail makes a short, but wet and rocky, descent to a rock-hop crossing of Proctor Branch. (A crossing is likely difficult after heavy rainfall.) Beyond the branch, the trail follows a nearly level old rail grade used by the Kitchen Lumber Company. But the easy walking is fool's gold. After the trail takes a hard left through Upper Flats backcountry campsite—site of a former logging camp—and crosses Greer Branch, it begins a steep, rocky climb for the next 2½ miles. The ascent of about two thousand feet in elevation to a delightful open area known as Rye Patch does not prove to be great fun in the muggy, buggy conditions. Splashing my face with water from a small branch provides some relief on the way up, and I do enjoy wildflowers such as fire pink and flame azalea, in addition to limited views of the Yellow Creek and Cheoah Mountains. But overall, the walking through here isn't particularly pleasant on a steamy summer day, especially where the trail is overgrown. Past Rye Patch (now populated mostly by ferns and weeds), however, I enjoy a basically level trail through a cooler forest for the remaining three-fourths mile or so to the eastern edge of Rich Gap. Through the trees to my left, I get a glimpse of Gregory and Parson Balds, the final two lofty sentinels of the Smokies' crest before the divide falls off sharply to Deals Gap at the far southwestern border of the park.

At Rich Gap, I turn left, or west, to follow Gregory Bald Trail for another three-fourths mile to the bald itself. A stiff climb begins just past the nearby junction with Gregory Ridge Trail, where a few hikers have gathered before making their final ascent up the mountain. I hurry past them, as I've long been ready to reach the main attraction.

I arrive on the bald about fifteen minutes later and begin to enjoy the brilliant, blooming flame azalea, as well as the distant views on this unusually clear June day. In order to enjoy the flowers and vistas even more, I wander around the bald on a few side trails—very cautiously, I might add, because the last time I was here I came upon the largest timber rattlesnake I've ever encountered. The rattler was likely about four feet long, with a thick body to boot. But no harm done.

As I meander I don't spot any creamy white or pale yellow azalea—or as many shrubs in bloom—as I did on previous visits. But the orange and red blossoms I do see are brilliant. And the views of high peaks such as Stratton and Hooper Balds, in the Unicoi Mountains to the southwest, are sublime. Because good sitting rocks on the North Carolina side of the bald are scarce at best, and I'm not interested in joining a chigger convention in the luxuriant mountain oat grass, I land on a nice resting spot in the crook of a gnarled tree. Alas, I'm soon obliged to move on after a trio of horseback riders chooses to ride down from their previous prime spot in a copse of trees, stopping directly in front of me.

A few years ago I decided to join, for an afternoon, the continuing work to keep Gregory Bald a bald by volunteering to help cut woody plants and other encroaching vegetation. Thus on a hot August day, I made the long, steep climb from Twentymile in order to meet a crew of park-service employees hiking up from the Tennessee side, who would provide brief training and tools, including chaps to provide rattlesnake protection. I arrived early in the afternoon according to plan and waited (one hour) . . . and waited (two hours) . . . and waited (three hours). Finally, abandoning my stubbornness, I headed back down to Twentymile, as the August daylight wouldn't last forever and I'm not a big fan of walking in the dark, even with a flashlight. I learned later from the supervisor that he was ill that day and that the work crew . . . well, it didn't quite make it to the bald on schedule. I readily concede, however, that there are worse places on the planet to hang around for three hours.

On this day, I depart Gregory Bald after about an hour, hiking down on the out-and-back route I took on my aborted volunteer day. I walk down a rocky section of Gregory Bald Trail to Sheep Pen Gap, like Upper Flats the location of another backcountry campsite currently closed because of aggressive black bear activity. At the gap, I turn left to pick up the Wolf Ridge Trail that takes me about 6¼ miles to the Twentymile Trail junction. The walking up to nearby Parson Bald is pleasant and easy, on a gentle grade. The bald has been overrun by vegetation that includes a scrubby mix of pine and oak trees. When I first visited here in the mid-1980s, there were still some good views to the southwest even in June; thirty years later, there are none this time of year. Farther down the trail, after it begins to descend sharply, I stop to rest on a rock outcrop and enjoy a cool breeze that is causing a sea of ferns to wave in the wind. I resume hiking, and soon I'm back in the thick of the lower-elevation heat and humidity, swatting gnats as I go. Over its final mile or so, Wolf Ridge Trail crosses the lovely Moore Springs Branch several times on foot logs, a couple of which are missing handrails. But the crossings are easy enough to negotiate, as none of them exceeds a dozen paces or so.

Arduous hiking notwithstanding, it's been another rewarding summer day in the higher terrain of the Great Smokies. It will be difficult, at least until the fall color of October, to match the spectacular array of hikes I've done this month. At mid-year I've completed twenty excursions, totaling slightly more than two hundred miles, on all or part of about three dozen trails in the Smokies. I'm aiming to double all three numbers by year's end.

Hike 21

Nirvana—Most of the Year

July 2
Trails: Thomas Divide,
   Newton Bald
*Trailhead weather
   conditions:* 58 degrees,
   sunny, calm
Round-trip miles hiked: 10.4

Today I bravely set out for the Smokies on another of the busiest weekends of the year. I reach the park early enough to see several elk grazing in the large field adjoining Oconaluftee Visitor Center. But I'm hoping the trail itself—perhaps my favorite section of trail in the entire park—won't be overrun with hikers and back packers. Horse travel shouldn't be an issue, since horses aren't allowed on the section, though I have seen hoof-prints on it. The path is the northern section of Thomas Divide Trail, with an upper trailhead located a few miles south of Newfound Gap. I've been on parts of the nearly fourteen-mile-long trail earlier this year, but not from the northern terminus that lies at about forty-six hundred feet in elevation. On this sunny summer day, I'll hike about five miles out before taking a left on Newton Bald Trail in order to reach Newton Bald backcountry campsite. I plan to clean up the camp for a third time this year—using a third different route—as part of my Smokies volunteer duties.

Named for mid-nineteenth century Cherokee chief and forceful tribal advocate William "Little Will" Thomas, Thomas Divide is a long, crescent-shaped ridge that extends from the Smokies' crest to the Deep Creek area. As a result, its elevation ranges from more than five thousand feet to less than two thousand. Although the trail that traces the ridge winds through heavily forested areas, the path does yield some impressive views when the deciduous trees are bare. Built by the Civilian Conservation Corps in 1934, the year the park was established, Thomas Divide Trail also features as fine a hiking tread on its upper five miles as any mountain trail I've ever hiked: generally soft footing, mostly free of rocks, roots, gullies, and muddy sections. It's hiking nirvana—except on ice or snow—on a well-graded trail.

As is often the case, the trailhead parking area is empty upon my arrival, though that will change soon enough on this holiday weekend. But only fifteen minutes out, as I rest briefly on a rotting log at a sharp bend in the trail, I'm surprised to see a middle-aged couple heading toward the trailhead I just departed. They say they hiked up Kanati Fork Trail, noting that its distance must be a mile longer than its published mileage of 2.9, before turning right in order to hike the 1.7 miles to Thomas Divide Trail's northern terminus. When I ask if someone is giving them a ride from the trailhead parking area to the Kanati Fork trailhead about five miles down Newfound Gap Road, they reply that they're planning to walk along the road to Kanati Fork. Even on a quiet weekend, I wouldn't wish to walk five miles along the main road through the park. But different strokes, I suppose.

Shafts of morning sunlight illuminate the forest's grassy floor as I make my way along the trail. On parts of the path I hear the distant roar of motorcycles on Newfound Gap Road, but it's mostly quiet—and still—in this high-elevation forest. I think about what a contrast these woods are to frenzied places such as Gatlinburg, Pigeon Forge, and even Sugarlands Visitor Center on a hectic holiday weekend. Suffice it to say, I'm grateful for this cool, green refuge that seems worlds apart.

Soon I arrive at the junction of Thomas Divide/ Kanati Fork Trails, situated in a broad, flat area that provides an uncommonly pleasant rest spot. A few red spruce are scattered among the northern hardwoods here, along with an old boar trap—tagged with the number 36—that's no longer baited or set to trip, as a stick is propping up the gate. As usual, there's a fresh breeze through here while I enjoy a quick snack and drink before hitting the trail again for the climb up to Nettle Creek Bald, a nearly mile-high summit that is Thomas Divide Trail's highest point. Like most named balds in the Smokies, Nettle Creek Bald is now forested, with limited views, despite its lofty elevation.

From the bald, I begin a steady descent of almost a mile to Tuskee Gap, roughly six hundred feet lower in elevation than Nettle Creek Bald. The trail narrows and hugs the ridge as it leans a bit in places, but the walking is still quite easy overall. I spot a few stray Rosebay rhododendron blooms on the way down, their creamy white blossoms adding another color to the green environs. After the broad swag of Tuskee Gap, I start climbing toward the next trail junction, this one with Sunkota Ridge Trail, which rises up from the Deep Creek area. At the junction, I recall an encounter I had a few years ago with a father and his young daughter and son. The dad noted that the three of them planned to hike the entire Mountains-to-Sea Trail across North Carolina, in phases, by the time the children finish high school. As I rest here today I wonder how much progress they have made toward that ambitious goal.

There's one more short climb leading up to the five-thousand-foot Newton Bald camp—today's destination and work site. On the way is the only sloppy section on the entire hike and it's a short one—a miry stretch fewer than ten feet long. Soon I reach the junction with Newton Bald Trail, where the trail sign notes that the campsite is two-tenths mile to the left. Actually the campsite is no more than one hundred yards of level trail from here, but no, I'm not complaining about the inaccurate distance after the climb from the Sunkota Trail junction.

The first order of business upon arriving at the campsite is to hang my pack on a food cable and check the spring about seventy-five yards down a steep side trail. I'm thinking that even with the extremely dry weather of the past several months, I'll find a good flow from the spring, because I've never seen it even close to running dry. I'm not disappointed; clear, cold water flows out of the ground as if being gently pumped. Moore Spring, on the eastern shoulder of Gregory Bald, has been touted as perhaps the finest spring in the Smokies, but it's doubtful that Moore or any other spring in the park surpasses this one for reliability. As always, I'm tempted to cup my hands and drink the water here, but there's the not-insignificant matter of viruses, bacteria, and the Giardia parasite to worry about with untreated water in the backcountry. I do, however, clean out some sediment and leaf debris and splash my face with the bracing water. Yes, it's gotten a bit warm by early afternoon, even at about five thousand feet.

As I finish cleaning up around the campsite's permanent fire ring, a couple of day hikers approach from Thomas Divide Trail; they've also planned an out-and-back hike from the upper trailhead. They're renting a mountain cabin for a month and ask where they should hike the following day. I suggest Hemphill Bald Trail along the park boundary because it's high elevation and near where they are staying. Soon, we're joined by two gregarious guys, also coming from the northern terminus, who have worked out a car switch so that they can walk down Newton Bald Trail to the Smokemont area. While I wrap up the rest of my work around the site, a solo day hiker arrives at the campsite; he and I talk later at the nearby trail junction with a couple of other hikers. A total of nine hikers in five different parties—I think that's probably a record for me on Thomas Divide Trail. But all were in good cheer on a superb day for hiking.

I start back toward the day's starting point and set a good pace until I begin the lengthy climb from Tuskee Gap to Nettle Creek Bald. As I stop to rest, I notice a few waning galax blooms. After topping the bald, I nearly step on a shrew crossing the trail, and then inadvertently disturb a maggot mass that I quickly walk past. At the junction of Kanati Fork Trail, the solo hiker reappears, and we chat for a couple of minutes before he turns right down that trail. I continue on Thomas Divide Trail, spotting some bear scat before I reach the knoll known as Turkey Flyup.

Soon I start to hear what sounds like heavy traffic along Newfound Gap Road, traffic I don't look forward to joining in just a few minutes. I then turn right on the trail in order to make the path's final descent. There's a glimpse or two of Clingmans Dome through the dense forest to my left, and as usual on this stretch, I start to whistle and then softly sing—perhaps I can call it singing—a few verses of the folk ballad "On Top of Old Smoky." Back at the parking area where I start to pull out, one of the car-switch guys I saw at Newton Bald campsite approaches my car on foot just to let me know they made it out safely. We shake hands, and I drive away after another sublime summer day on Thomas Divide.

Hike 22

Heeding Heintooga's Call

July 4
Trail: Flat Creek
*Trailhead weather
conditions:* 69 degrees,
partly cloudy, breezy
Round-trip miles hiked: 5.6

Most summers since the mid-1980s, Karen and I have celebrated Independence Day high in the Great Smoky Mountains, at one of our favorite spots: Heintooga Picnic Area and Overlook. The setting for the picnic ground, more than a mile high and developed by the Civilian Conservation Corps, is unsurpassed on a summer day. The tables and grills, which are plentiful but never heavily used, are situated in a cool, dark forest of tall spruce and hardwood trees. We've visited on the Fourth when temperatures reached the upper nineties in the valleys, yet we still felt cool in the shade of Heintooga's stately trees. Except for fresh breezes that sway those trees, the picnic area is usually cathedral quiet. We even have a favorite table we aim for on our picnics, which features a large stone-slab top as do several others nearby. Although we continue to enjoy each visit to Heintooga, the most memorable outings will always be those during the wonder years when our sons were little guys, eagerly awaiting food cooked on the grill as they explored the area around the picnic table. What great times those were.

And then there's the spectacular Heintooga Overlook, just a couple of dozen paces down from the picnic area. Located fewer than two hundred yards from the start of Flat Creek Trail, the overlook affords a commanding view of about 70 percent of the Great Smokies' crest when skies are relatively clear. From the lookout, one can see the Smokies' three loftiest summits: Mount Guyot to the right, on the eastern end of the Smokies' divide; Mount Le Conte straight ahead, rising up just beyond the divide; and elevation king Clingmans Dome to the far left. It's a truly remarkable vantage point, with its sweeping views of waves and waves of bluish distant ridges with soft, green mountains closer in.

On this July 4, we won't be grilling anything, but we've brought hefty sandwiches to enjoy at our favorite table after we finish today's hike on the short Flat Creek Trail. The trail starts from a large parking circle at the end of Heintooga Ridge Road, just before the graveled, one-way Balsam Mountain Road begins a serpentine journey of nearly twenty miles toward the Big Cove community on the Cherokee Indian Reservation. Nearby, a few steps from the road itself, is the trailhead for the even shorter (less than a mile) Balsam Mountain Nature Trail that connects the picnic area with cozy Balsam Mountain Campground. At 5,310 feet of elevation, this is easily the highest developed campground in the park. Upon our mid-afternoon arrival at the parking circle, we see only two cars parked there—even fewer than usual on the Fourth for this remote area.

Flat Creek Trail begins its 2.6-mile course on a wide, flat roadbed that reaches Heintooga Overlook after just a couple of minutes of walking. Rarely does so little effort on a trail result in so big a payoff as the short walk to the overlook. Typical summertime clouds and slightly hazy skies reduce the views today, yet we don't feel the least bit cheated with the broad vista we see. Although we'll return to this Eden at the conclusion of our hike, we're obliged to stop in awe right now and take a few photos.

After a few minutes, we resume walking on Flat Creek Trail, making a short initial descent through a mile-high forest of red spruce and northern hardwoods.

After skirting Flat Creek Bald, the trail briefly levels before we begin another fairly significant descent. We then enter a, yes, mostly flat area, in which there are five easy crossings of Flat Creek, a stream that comes by its name honestly through here. Lush grass, almost surreally green, flanks the trail on either side as we relish the quiet of the forest; on the entire hike we'll see only one other couple. Rising up from the forest floor like so many white-topped spires is a profusion of black snakeroot, a.k.a. black cohosh. We enjoy easy walking through an area that seems specifically designed to melt earthly concerns.

Soon we reach the site of an old camp that's long since been removed from the Smokies' backcountry roster, likely a wise move considering the usual wetness of the area. Today, however, the trail and surrounding woods are drier than I've ever seen them. Just beyond the old campsite is a short side trail that leads down to Flat Creek Falls, where Flat Creek finally takes a sharp tumble off a ridge toward a meeting with Bunches Creek. We turn right onto the side trail, stepping or sliding over a few blowdowns as we continue down the path toward the falls. Alas, a split in the trail near the creek offers mainly rocky, overgrown routes rather than good views of the falls. Even so, we don't regret trying to see what we could of the creek where it abruptly loses its flatness.

Back on the main trail, we swing away from Flat Creek and soon begin descending toward easy crossings of Bunches Creek and one of its tributaries, crossings that are well above the confluence of Flat and Bunches Creeks. After the second one, we have a moderately steep ascent to the paved parking area along Heintooga Ridge Road, where Flat Creek Trail's lower terminus is located. Although there are no cars or vehicle traffic here as we arrive, we don't linger long as we're eager to return to the real attractions of the day: Heintooga Overlook and Picnic Area.

It's a pleasant woodland walk back toward the picnic ground, and a generally gradual one, even with the two rather stiff ascents near the end. A welcome breeze freshens as we approach the overlook on a day that is seventy degrees even up high. I continue on to the parking area to retrieve our small cooler and make my way back up to our favorite rock table. No little boys and no charcoal fire today, but it's still a wonderful place to eat, while we recall so many happy outings.

After picnicking, we're compelled to walk back down to Heintooga Overlook, where each of the three benches—serving as sort of a grandstand for viewing the Smokies—is empty. Karen stretches out on one, I on another as we settle in to watch fast-moving clouds and ever-changing light from this magnificent lookout. With no other visitors for a while (some Balsam Mountain campers will no doubt arrive for sunset), we rest mostly in silence as a long summer day begins to fade. Periodically, I refer to a Smokies trail map, or look at the lofty horizon through binoculars. But mostly, I just gaze in wonder at ancient mountains that people less than a century ago had the foresight, goodwill, and determination to preserve for future generations. Yes, there will be fireworks viewing later on from an overlook several miles away along Heintooga Ridge Road, but no show can compare with this natural one from Heintooga Overlook.

Hike 23

A Rocky Road

July 10
Trails: Road Prong, Chimney Tops
Trailhead weather conditions: 62 degrees, high clouds, slight breeze
Round-trip miles hiked: 7.0

On another dry summer day, with a slim chance of storms even at high elevations, I decide to hike two trails on the northern (Tennessee) side of the Smokies' crest: Road Prong and Chimney Tops. Each is spectacular, not to mention difficult, in its own way. Partly because it shapes up as an outing for which sure footing is imperative, I choose to wear heavier, sturdier boots today as opposed to the light hikers I've relied on most of the year. That proves to be a good call.

The trailhead for today's excursion is located at Indian Gap, not quite two miles west of Newfound Gap, along Clingmans Dome Road. The mighty Appalachian Trail runs through the gap, just above the trailhead for Road Prong Trail, which works its way northwest from Indian Gap. The latter trail then turns almost due north to meet Chimney Tops Trail after about 2½ mostly rocky, slippery miles. It's a beautiful, but often wet and treacherous, route that actually merges with the stream in several places.

Though perhaps little known or noticed these days, Indian Gap actually has a fair amount of human history. Difficult as it is to believe today, the main route over the rugged Smokies traveled through this gap well into the twentieth century. In the early 1830s, the North Carolina General Assembly authorized the Oconaluftee Turnpike Company to build a road to the gap that mostly followed an old Indian trace. As one might imagine, the road—a path, really—was not exactly a modern highway. Its primary initial purpose was to enable the driving of livestock to market. Although the path into Tennessee was upgraded to a wagon road during the Civil War, it remained a difficult and narrow route for any type of traffic. Finally, a century after the Oconaluftee Turnpike was authorized, a modern highway for horseless carriages was completed before the 1934 establishment of Great Smoky Mountains National Park: Newfound Gap Road (a.k.a. U.S. 441). Today, it remains the only road crossing the Smokies' crest. As it turned out, the elevation of the newly found gap was more than two hundred feet lower than that of the almost exactly mile-high Indian Gap.

These days, the Road Prong Trail, which quickly descends from the gap, is limited to foot traffic, and for good reason. Tricky enough in places even for hikers, the trail would surely stymie anything other than foot travel. Anyone taking on the trail should have good balance; sturdy boots that can handle some creek water; and the ability to follow the trail in and out of the stream. That said, the trail does offer thrilling, if sometimes forbidding, beauty along with its real challenges. Among the lovely flowers in bloom on this July day are Rosebay rhododendron, Turk's Cap Lily, and Oswego tea, or bee balm.

I start out on the trail early in the day and almost immediately begin a sharp descent on loose rocks, as the path follows a course wedged between Sugarland Mountain and Mingus Lead (leading, by the way, to fifty-eight-hundred-foot Mount Mingus). But the footing is fine compared with what I'll encounter a bit farther down the trail. There's a large blowdown blocking the path, but the detour around it is short and easily negotiated. It's quiet walking through this boreal forest until rushing Road Prong pops up to the left of the trail,

a prong that anyone hiking this trail becomes quite familiar with soon enough.

After about one half-mile of hiking, I catch up to a large group of hikers just starting a wet crisscrossing of Road Prong. I'm obliged to wait a minute or so behind the trailing hiker, who is nonchalantly blocking my progress as he takes pictures along the narrow path leading into the stream. After emerging on *terra firma* a couple of minutes later, I think about how this path is the antithesis of Thomas Divide Trail and its mostly soft, sure footing. If I don't fall on my backside on Road Prong Trail today, it certainly won't be for lack of opportunities.

At a trail crossing of a small tributary tumbling toward the stream, I continue on what looks and feels like an actual path. Here, I enjoy a nice view of the prong from high above. But quickly, the trail kisses the prong again and travels through standing water to the right of the stream, water that was likely deposited by flash flooding. Yes, water is a core feature of the aptly named Road Prong Trail.

The conditions become muggy and still as I travel past Indian Grave Flats. The site is named for a Cherokee Indian buried by Confederate troops after Union soldiers mortally wounded him. Several lovely cascades are the reward for my negotiating three major blowdowns and a wide, hazardous stream crossing. And no, there's no foot log at the fording of the prong, contrary to one being noted in at least one recently published trail guide. I soon arrive at Beech Flats and the intersection with Chimney Tops Trail. The latter seems like a pedestrian freeway—in both width and traffic—compared with Road Prong Trail. I turn left toward the ever-popular Chimneys, which yields dramatic, rocky lookouts that draw big crowds most anytime of year.

On a July morning, I'm surprised not to see anyone on Chimney Tops Trail for even a minute or two, because the short, steep trail attracts tens of thousands of hikers annually. But I don't get far before the waves of hikers begin—initially a young couple coming down the trail, followed by larger groups who apparently got off the mark early from the trailhead along Newfound Gap Road. I have slightly more than a mile of mostly sharp climbing (gaining, in fact, an elevation of about one thousand feet) on Chimney Tops Trail before I reach the dramatic, rocky pinnacles known as the Chimneys.

Like the Forney Ridge Trail I hiked in June, extensive trail rehabilitation has vastly improved Chimney Tops Trail in recent years, making the steep climb to the Chimneys considerably easier and more enjoyable. How extensive? Nearly four hundred rock steps were laid during the rehabbing. Almost three hundred locust log steps were constructed. And about seven hundred square feet of retaining walls were built. Completed in 2015, the $450,000 project—funded by the Trails Forever endowment—took about three years to finish. The labor-intensive transformation of the formerly rocky and, in some places, badly eroded trail is impressive, to say the least.

As I start ascending in earnest via those rock and log steps, the valley, which is creased by a tributary of Road Prong, begins to resemble a ravine more than a valley. The climb is unrelenting until a switchback swings the trail to the left, followed in short order by another that sends the trail back to the right on a northerly course toward the Chimneys. From this point, I find the climbing mostly moderate, not unlike many well-graded trails in the Smokies. At a clearing, there's a fine view of both Mingus Lead and Sugarland Mountain, the two towering ridges flanking Road Prong Trail. I'm closing in on the Chimneys.

I round a bend in the trail, where the path briefly becomes miry, and enjoy a straight-on view of the soaring Chimney pinnacles that are such an attraction. (*Footnote:* Tragically, this area is where a devastating fire will be intentionally started later in the year.) Hikers are coming and going as the trail soon gives way to a steep rock face leading to the summit. I make my way about one-third of the way up, then peel off to a small shelf to the right in order to allow several hikers to ease their way back down the rock. It's slow going and precarious for hikers ascending and descending, with most people going up on all fours and most coming down inching along on their backsides. Because of the continuing heavy traffic, I decide to eat one of my sandwiches instead of proceeding farther up the rocky route myself. I climbed to the top sometime in the 1980s and figure I don't need to repeat that feat today at age sixty-four.

As I carefully work back down the rock face from my lunch spot, I steady myself on the trunk of a Fraser fir and end up with sticky, but aromatic, resin on my hand. Near the end of my descent, a young woman tells her friends that a chipmunk is scampering about. I can't resist blurting out that the animal is actually "a red squirrel, called a boomer." I hope she—and they—didn't think I was too much of a wise guy.

Hike 24

Along the High Boundary

July 23
Trail: Cataloochee Divide
*Trailhead weather
   conditions:* 72 degrees,
   partly cloudy, calm
Round-trip miles hiked: 9.0

Cataloochee Divide is one of the lofty ridges that walls off pastoral Cataloochee Valley from the rest of the world. It also mostly marks the southeastern boundary of Great Smoky Mountains National Park. The path that follows the divide from Cove Creek Gap, the aptly named Cataloochee Divide Trail, is the trail of choice today on a ninety-degree day in the valleys. Although the trailhead is the only one in the park I can reach from my house in an hour, getting there does involve driving several miles on the narrow, winding road accessed via U.S. 276, near Interstate 40. I'm especially looking forward to today's excursion because for the first time this year, son Ben and his wife, Ashley Miller, are joining Karen and me on what should be a fun family outing along the high divide. But we will likely need some good fortune to dodge afternoon thunderstorms, which can certainly pose problems for hikers on ridgetops.

Oddly enough, upon our arrival at the park boundary where the trailhead is located, we see a parked horse-drawn carriage with a friendly fellow inside, but no parked automobiles. Even on a Saturday in July, we're going to have Cataloochee Divide Trail to ourselves. Although the four-thousand-foot-elevation gap is definitely cooler than the valleys, it's nonetheless still and warm at the trailhead in late morning. Directly across the road from our trailhead is the Asbury Trail, which Methodist Episcopal Bishop Francis Asbury traveled as part of his extensive circuit-riding journeys in the early nineteenth century. Although not part of the current Smokies' trail system, the Asbury Trail is still used by some recreational hikers.

As with many trails on the North Carolina side of the park, I have something of a history with Cataloochee Divide Trail, one of my favorite paths most anytime of year. Sometime in the 1980s, about three miles from the trailhead, I came upon a black bear for the first time on any trail. The animal took off in a rush, as has been my experience on subsequent bear encounters almost without exception. On that same hike, I saw what appeared to be a dead bobcat in the middle of the trail. A turkey vulture was picking it apart, and I didn't quite have the stomach to inspect the carcass in order to confirm that it was indeed a bobcat. Today we'll spot a few wild turkeys, but no vultures.

It doesn't take long for us to see one of the loveliest of July wildflowers, Turk's Cap Lily, as the trail hugs the park boundary to our left. The boundary is delineated in places by a battered split-rail fence, along with some barbed wire. The path itself is easy on the feet, with few rocky or muddy places, at least as far as our one-way route of slightly more than four miles out. There's also not a great deal of climbing, or descending for that matter, until the fourth mile of hiking. Along the way, we see a few rock outcrops—a couple of which are big enough to provide decent shelter from a storm—as well as some large northern hardwoods that appear to be old growth.

Just as he did as a little boy, young Ben (who has just turned twenty-nine) asks a lot of good questions—most of which I can answer, some with an assist from Karen—about flora, fauna, and the park itself as we proceed along the trail. After about a half hour of pleasant walking and conversation, we reach a small clearing to the right of the trail that affords what is surely one of the East's finest wilderness views. None of the vast, mountainous terrain we see from here is inhabited by humans; the heavily forested land all lies within the park. Especially prominent are the 5,647-foot Spruce Mountain, looming high along the mighty Balsam Mountain Range, and towering Mount Sterling Ridge. We can also see a small piece of Cataloochee Valley, which is more than fifteen hundred feet lower than we are at this lookout. The Cherokee had a name for the waves and waves of mountains we're now admiring: *Ga-da-lu-tsi*, loosely translated as "standing in a row." European settlers eventually transformed the name to Cataloochee.

We resume walking and soon begin a significant descent to the trail's next notable landmark, which is just beyond a private residence perched outside the park boundary. Panther Spring Gap lies slightly more than two miles out, where a private dirt road parallels the boundary. Legend has it that a panther dragged a young girl, alive and screaming, across the gap into Cataloochee Valley. Although there are still occasional reports of panthers in Cataloochee and elsewhere in the Smokies, the animal is generally thought to be extirpated from these mountains, gone the way of the bison.

In another mile or so, we reach a way station of sorts, where there's a clearing and a sturdy wooden shelter on the privately owned side of the fence line. From this spot, there's an unobstructed view of Purchase Knob, which looms above the divide at an elevation of 5,086 feet. The knob rises directly across from today's destination, the Appalachian Highlands Science Learning Center, which is part of the park. Although the hiking hasn't been difficult to this point, this spot is a good place to regroup because the trail is about to begin climbing in earnest as it works its way toward the learning center. The center is part of a network of centers that support research and science education in our national parks.

After our short break, the easy hiking soon gives way to a steep section of trail that is briefly rocky, muddy, and overgrown in places. Although the mile or so stretch isn't terribly demanding, it's a definite contrast to the first three miles of the trail. We climb to about five thousand feet before the path bends and levels. Soon Ashley spots a faint trail and small sign to the left that indicates no horse travel, but we decide to continue a short distance on the main trail until it reaches a more heavily used connecting trail to the learning center. From here, it's an easy quarter-mile walk to the grassy, wide-open area where the handsome center is located. Aside from Purchase Knob itself, the most prominent peak is the nearly mile-high Sandymush Bald, which crowns the Newfound Mountains, outside the park on the far side of I-40. (The Newfound Mountains should not be confused with distant Newfound Gap, in the heart of the Smokies.)

The Appalachian Highlands Science Learning Center and its surrounding 535 acres are part of the park because of the generosity of Kathryn McNeil and Voit Gilmore, a San Francisco couple who donated the land to the federal government in 2000. They could have made a very tidy sum by selling the land or by developing it into a gated residential community with a name like The Meadows at Purchase Knob. Instead, the beautiful tract where the center was built is now part of the park. A historic cabin sits on the tract, as well as a web cam and a weather/air-quality monitoring station. As for the center itself, its research and education facilities include lodging, a meeting room, and a wet lab.

We land on steps and a bench on the shaded side of the learning center and dig into our lunch sandwiches. As we eat, we enjoy a nice cooling breeze in addition to the wonderful surroundings. Several young students from Great Smoky Mountains Institute at Tremont, which is based inside the park near Townsend, Tennessee, soon join us. It's difficult to imagine a more pleasant place for all of us to have lunch on a warm summer day.

After taking a few pictures, we start back toward Cataloochee Divide Trail. This time, we turn right on the faint path Ashley noticed earlier and it does prove to be a slight shortcut back to the main trail. The return trip, mostly downhill except for the short climb from Panther Spring Gap, goes considerably faster than the hike out. Best of all, we don't get hammered by an afternoon thunderstorm. We do stop a few times to admire the views and wildflowers, including the chlorophyll-lacking Indian pipe, but otherwise we set a good pace. We all agree we probably could not have asked for a better summertime outing in our nearby national park. Thank you again, Messrs. Rockefeller, Roosevelt, et al. . . . and, from this century, Ms. McNeil and Mr. Gilmore. Let's hope your contributions to the public good endure well beyond the lives of those of us who are currently enjoying them.

Hike 25

Cataloochee Divide (Continued)

August 12
Trail: Hemphill Bald
Trailhead weather conditions: 63 degrees, sunny, calm
Round-trip miles hiked: 9.6

After hiking the northeastern section of Cataloochee Divide on my previous outing, today I decide to hike the opposite end of the divide, traveling at least as far as 5,540-foot Hemphill Bald. Apparently that destination provided the rationale some years ago for renaming the southwestern part of the path Hemphill Bald Trail. As with Cataloochee Divide Trail, Hemphill Bald Trail mostly hugs the park boundary until it drops to Double Gap on the far side of the bald. There it turns left, descending rather sharply to Caldwell Fork in Cataloochee Valley. At one time, that latter section of Hemphill Bald Trail was known as Double Gap Trail, but the Hemphill moniker has also overtaken that trail name. Cataloochee Divide Trail follows the high divide from Double Gap. After about one-half mile, the trail passes The Swag resort, which borders the park, on the way to Cove Creek Gap (Hike 24 trailhead) more than six miles away.

According to the venerable *Farmers' Almanac*, the dog days of summer ended yesterday, twenty days after the alignment of Sirius (a.k.a. Dog Star) with the sun. But if popular usage of the term is accurate when referencing hot, dry weather, thus far August in the Great Smokies hasn't measured up. As is often the case in August, it was difficult to plan a long, relatively dry hike for most of the month to date, as a stubborn weather pattern produced flash flooding in some streams and flood watches across the mountains. The Smokies don't have an actual monsoon, but this month's persistently soggy conditions seem to belie that fact. Although today's weather forecast isn't particularly promising either, I decide that twelve days into the month is plenty long enough to wait before setting out on my first excursion in August. Fair weather and hiking in the Great Smoky Mountains obviously don't always coincide.

The Hemphill Bald trailhead is located slightly more than six miles out on Heintooga Ridge Road, a spur of the Blue Ridge Parkway that begins near mile marker 458. Heintooga Ridge Road enters the park after about 3½ miles, at Black Camp Gap, before it reaches the trailhead parking at Polls Gap. Rough Fork Trail, heading down into Cataloochee Valley, also starts from the parking area. A third trail, Polls Gap, formerly began at the same lot, but the path—plagued by erosion and blowdowns—is no longer even occasionally maintained. Although a wooden sign at the trailhead notes the trail is only temporarily closed, Polls Gap Trail was removed from the official Smokies' trail map quite some time ago. As I recall from a hike in the 1980s, the somewhat overgrown path wasn't especially enjoyable to hike anyway.

After spotting several elk cows and wild turkeys on the high-elevation drive along Heintooga Ridge Road, I find Polls Gap a surprisingly busy place upon my arrival in early morning. Not only are several cars parked at the gap, but a park-service employee is mowing the grass around the parking area. After he waves me on, I slowly drive around his trailer to park in one of the two remaining spots in the paved lot. A couple of minutes later, he finishes mowing and walks over to engage in friendly conversation before he moves on to his next work site. It's always heartening to talk with longtime park-service employees who still love their jobs despite (because of?) the challenges they face.

The sky is October blue as I set out on Hemphill Bald Trail shortly before nine o'clock. At the outset, the trail is nearly tabletop flat as it follows an old rail grade, a vestige of the intense logging operations of the Suncrest Lumber Company that leveled many a fine tree in the Smokies before the park was born. I soon walk through a few rocky seeps, oozing across the trail, before I arrive at Garretts Gap slightly less than 1½ miles out. At the broad gap, the remnants of a split-rail fence built by the Civilian Conservation Corps mark part of the park boundary. Cutleaf coneflower blooms in profusion here, just outside the park.

From Garretts Gap, I begin a moderate climb as the trail swings around Buck Knob, which straddles the park boundary. I soon meet a solo hiker near a point where a park ranger was on a stakeout for ginseng poachers the last time I hiked the trail. The hiker is puzzled that he hasn't seen a sign or a marker for Cataloochee Divide, which the trailhead sign indicates is 1½ miles out. Actually the divide does begin around Garretts Gap, where Hemphill Bald Trail turns northwest as it departs Balsam Mountain, but the spot isn't marked. We part ways and soon, at a small break in the thick foliage, I get a glimpse to the north of soaring Mount Sterling Ridge and its tallest peak, 6,155-foot-high Big Cataloochee Mountain.

After bypassing Buck Knob, I follow the trail on a gradual descent to the unappealingly named Maggot Spring Gap. Fortunately, the gap is a much pleasanter place than its name indicates, enhanced this morning by a cooling breeze as the temperature approaches seventy. At this point, the trail is about to begin a more significant climb, employing a half-dozen or so switchbacks to reach the crest of Sheepback Knob at about fifty-five hundred feet. I see a sad sight through a slight opening in the trees: acres and acres of dead hemlock trees on Shanty Mountain, victims of the hemlock woolly adelgid that has wreaked havoc in the Smokies and elsewhere. If the chestnut blight was one of the great ecological tragedies of the twentieth century, a twenty-first century counterpart is the hemlock woolly adelgid. Although the National Park Service has halted some of the non-native pest's destructive march across the Smokies by using chemical and biological treatments in some areas, the alarming fact is that more than 85 percent of the park's great hemlock forests are declining. The results, including the impact on trout streams cooled by the shade of hemlocks, are nothing short of devastating and widespread. For example, the one-way Parson Branch Road, leading from the Cades Cove area to U.S. 129, closed indefinitely in 2016 because of its high concentration of dead or dying hemlock trees. A staggering total of seventeen hundred hazardous trees were identified within falling distance of the eight-mile-long road, or more than two hundred per linear road mile. And that's just along the road corridor.

Farther along the trail, at roughly the same elevation as Sheepback Knob, is Little Bald Knob. After leaving Little Bald for a somewhat lengthy descent to Pine Tree Gap, I notice a short side trail to the right that leads to a fine view outside the park of Moody Top, standing guard over the town of Maggie Valley. As I near Pine Tree Gap, the fence marking the park boundary features what appears to be fresh barbed wire. In a couple of minutes, I see the reason for that. Several head of cattle are grazing on the privately owned Cataloochee Ranch side of the fence, doing their part to keep the area around Hemphill Bald open. I also spot a couple of red spruce around the gap, but curiously no pines, despite its name. As with the trailhead at Polls Gap, the elevation here is less than fifty-two hundred feet, meaning I have some climbing to do before topping Hemphill Bald in slightly more than a half-mile. I rest briefly on a log, enjoying a snack and water, before starting the ascent.

I pass several horseback riders, who have stopped at a hitching post on the ranch side of the boundary, then continue past a fence stile. Nearby, several hikers have congregated around a rock-table memorial to Tom and Judy Alexander, who founded Cataloochee Ranch about the time the park was established. In the 1990s, their family placed more than two hundred Hemphill Bald acres in a conservation easement, ensuring that the bald area won't be developed. I continue walking the trail to a gate, which also allows entry onto the bald and settle on a bench near a hitching post, amid prodigious cow patties. Even with a stubborn cloud bank directly in front of me, I see outstanding views of the Plott Balsam Mountains and their cloud-capped ridges to the south. In a few minutes, the sun pops through the nearby cloud bank, and I enjoy a close-up view of Jonathan Creek Valley about twenty-five hundred feet lower than where I'm perched. The breeze freshens, as it often does on this windswept bald, causing the air to feel cooler than the seventy-degree temperature on this mid-August day.

After talking for a couple of minutes with hikers from Texas and Florida—yes, flatlanders understandably are out in force here during the summer—I begin the hike back to Polls Gap. Although today's weather forecast included a good chance of showers, I stay dry all the way back to the car. Near the trailhead, I spot the tail of a white-tailed deer scampering away, the first wildlife I've seen on the trail today. It's been a pleasant, rain-free excursion on the southwestern section of Cataloochee Divide—the highest, longest ridge forming any part of the vast park boundary

Hike 26

A Great Smokies Grandstand

August 22
Trail: Appalachian
Trailhead weather
conditions: 68 degrees,
partly cloudy, calm
Round-trip miles hiked: 9.2

Although barely exceeding four thousand feet in elevation, the cone-shaped mountain colorfully known as Shuckstack has long had a reputation for providing one of the finest vantage points in the entire park. Nearly a half-mile lower in altitude than some other peaks in the Smokies, Shuckstack compensates for that deficiency by rising well above a relatively low-elevation neighborhood, which includes sprawling Fontana Lake. The lake was created by the damming of the Little Tennessee River during World War II. Thus, its stunning vistas are basically all about location, loca . . . aw, you know the rest. There's also an aging fire tower that gives a major boost to Shuckstack's long-range views. At the top of a stiff climb on the Appalachian Trail after the trail crosses Fontana Dam, Shuckstack serves as a sort of welcome to the Smokies for AT "thru-hikers" heading north, since you can see much of the park, including the soaring Smokies' crest, from its summit.

Partly because the trailhead for the shortest route to Shuckstack is a two-hour drive from our house, Karen and I decide to stay a couple of nights at nearby Fontana Village Resort, in the scenic cove where thousands of Fontana Dam construction workers lived from 1942 to 1944. Working three shifts a day, they completed the tallest dam in the East in slightly less than three years—a fast-and-furious wartime schedule undertaken in order to provide hydroelectric power for Oak Ridge and Alcoa in Tennessee. The hike from the trailhead is not even four miles one-way, but with an elevation gain of well over two thousand feet it can seem about twice that distance. Yes, Appalachian Trail hikers lugging heavy backpacks: welcome indeed to the Great Smoky Mountains.

Has it really been more than thirty years since I last hiked to Shuckstack? If memory serves, it actually was on a chilly day about a week into 1985. I was just a kid then—well, not really, because you're not a kid at thirty-three according to the lament in "Good Time Charlie's Got the Blues." But at that time, I was barely halfway to my current number of years and probably sure that I would return to Shuckstack in no more than three years rather than more than thirty. That lengthy absence from the mountain has certainly whetted my appetite for today's long-delayed return, arduous hiking notwithstanding.

After being restricted to foot traffic early in 2016, the road across the top of Fontana Dam reopened to vehicles in the spring. Even so, I decide to walk the nearly half-mile across the dam, following the route of the Appalachian Trail. From the far side of the dam it's still slightly more than a half-mile to a trailhead parking area where the AT slips back into the woods. By choosing not to park here, I've added about two miles round-trip to today's hike. But distance isn't the issue with a hike to Shuckstack; elevation gain is.

Also at the parking area, to the right of the AT section leading to Shuckstack, is the western trailhead for Lakeshore Trail, which snakes along the North Shore of Fontana Lake for nearly thirty-five miles. Initially the trail follows the old roadbed for N.C. 288, a high-

way abandoned by the state after much of it was flooded by the creation of Fontana Lake. In contrast to the park's Lake View Drive—commonly called The Road to Nowhere by local residents because the federal government never finished the promised road to replace N.C. 288—Lakeshore Trail is not The Trail to Nowhere; it continues all the way to Lake View Drive near Bryson City.

But today's destination, attained via a nearly bone-dry section of the twenty-two-hundred-mile Appalachian Trail, is the formidable Shuckstack. It's a destination that must be earned—there's no easy way to the top of the mountain, whose profile from a distance supposedly resembles that of a towering stack of corn-stalks. Now it's time for me to take it on again after a three-decade absence.

Veering to the left from the pavement, I rediscover that this piece of the AT wastes no time in beginning the ascent to Shuckstack. (After walking with me across the dam to this point, Karen doubles back to spend time on Fontana Lake.) But I also find that the trail is generally well graded with switchbacks, and that the path levels—even descends—in a few places. Its long-held reputation as an unrelenting killer hike may owe to a couple of factors: a stiff climb up Little Shuckstack, before a trail relocation bypassed the higher Shuckstack's two-hundred-foot-lower little brother; and AT hikers who may have gotten a little too content enjoying modern-day comforts for a day or two in and around Fontana Village, a resort for the past seventy years. No doubt many thru-hikers would take issue with that latter thought, advanced by someone they might dismiss as a tenderfoot with a relatively light daypack.

The woods are dead silent for a few minutes until I

hear the distant roar of motorcycles on N.C. 28 (*not* the old 288) and the hum of motorboats on Fontana Lake. Soon, I reach a rock outcrop that seems designed as a rest stop; there's even a flat rock jutting horizontally above ground that provides a nice seat. It's a good place to enjoy a snack and a drink of water before the trail resumes its climb toward the Shuckstacks.

As I continue a steady ascent, I encounter four backpackers on their way down from Shuckstack. I ask about the condition of the eighty-year-old fire tower and learn that although a handrail along the first flight of steps is missing, the tower itself is sturdy enough to climb. That's all the encouragement I need to even more eagerly anticipate my first trip to the top in more than thirty years. As I recall, the summit itself yielded some fine winter views, but I'm thinking that summertime foliage—especially three decades later—will be extremely limiting at ground level. Soon the trail takes a hard left at a draw where the trail has been relocated, leading to a large slate outcrop that yields magnificent views of several mountain ranges to the south and southwest.

The hike redeems its reputation as a thigh burner shortly after the outcrop, climbing steeply for about one-third mile up Twentymile Ridge to a junction where the mighty AT falls off rather meekly to the left toward Sassafras Gap and Twentymile and Lost Cove Trails. (The latter path connects with Lakeshore Trail, thereby enabling a long-loop hike back to the parking area at that trail's western trailhead.) The side trail to Shuckstack's smallish crown continues straight ahead, following a steep, rocky course for about 150 yards. Along with a rogue fire ring at the summit are a chimney and cistern, vestiges of a warden's cabin that was removed in the 1980s. Just a few steps away is the sixty-foot fire tower, one of four in the park that hasn't been dismantled, even though it's been decades since any of them have been used for their original purpose. And, yes, af-ter catching my breath for a couple of minutes, I plan to climb all the way to the top of the tower, which I will gladly have to myself.

Built in the mid-1930s by the Public Works Administration, Shuckstack fire tower is a landmark in the southwestern corner of the park, doggedly looming about twenty-three hundred feet above Fontana Lake. It has certainly seen better days. But the steel structure, its five landings, and its more than six dozen steps do, in fact, seem sound enough to ascend, though I might think otherwise if the wind were howling. Fortunately, there's just a slight breeze on this spectacular August day.

Up, up, up I go—to the final landing, then up the final few steps to the fire tower's cab, where the warden watched for fires. Unlike the steps and landings, the rotting floor doesn't seem safe, despite the fact that some plywood has been placed over the top of it. Not surprisingly, the cab is also extremely musty, not to mention a bit creepy. I quickly leave it and decide to sit on a step between the cab and the final landing. It's a safe, comfortable spot where the air really is fresh and sweet.

Words fall woefully short in any attempt to describe the 360-degree views from here, especially with such good visibility for an August afternoon. Suffice it to say that whoever first labeled Shuckstack the grandstand of the Great Smokies was dead on target. On my lofty perch, I eat lunch, and then take photos in different directions with a cell phone and digital camera that I carefully handle this high in the sky. Next, I break out the binoculars so I can bring the surrounding landmarks into closer view. Below me to the south, I see the 480-foot-tall Fontana Dam, along with much of Fontana Lake and its 238 miles of shoreline to the southeast. I can see a slice of another lake, Cheoah, to the southwest, along with Tennessee foothills in the far distance, thanks to a slight break in the mountains.

But the big attractions are the waves and waves of mountains inside and outside the park. The Smokies' highest peak, Clingmans Dome, is clearly visible to the northeast. Prominent several miles closer is fifty-five-hundred-foot Thunderhead, and closer still on the Smokies' crest is Gregory Bald at just under five thousand feet in elevation. Almost due east, rising along Welch Ridge, is the nearly mile-high High Rocks, where another old fire tower stood before its removal decades ago. Beyond the park, I can easily spot a number of mountain ranges, among them the Unicoi, Snowbird, Nantahala, Yellow Creek, and Cowee Mountains. Alone at the top of the tower on a gorgeous summer day, it feels as if I fleetingly own an embarrassment of panoramic riches.

After a while, it's time to slowly descend the steps to the base of the tower, because, after all, I'm not a forest-fire warden who has been pressed back into service. Back on *terra firma*, I drink some water before hitting the trail again. The trip down the AT goes quickly, though I do stop for a few minutes at the rock outcrop and again farther down. Ironically, after reaching the road, I spot my first wildlife of the day: a white-tailed deer prancing away, just as one did near the end of my previous hike to Hemphill Bald.

As I complete this sublime late-summer outing, the one hundredth anniversary of the National Park Service is just around the corner on August 25. Among those who likely will not be celebrating are surviving former residents (and perhaps many of their descendants) of land that is now flooded or isolated by Fontana Lake. I understand that sentiment; the weighty hand of the federal government can seem like an indiscriminate sledgehammer to people who are displaced from their homes, especially with no ready access to family cemeteries. But as a conservationist and United States citizen, I cannot say that the creation of Great Smoky Mountains National Park and Fontana Dam should not have happened, despite the sad displacement of many people via eminent domain. And the difficulty of those diasporas clearly pales when measured against the infamous Trail of Tears removal of the Cherokee to the Oklahoma Territory a century earlier, a far-reaching tragedy that cannot be defended. Although the greater good is not always easy to ascertain, I think it did prevail with the building of both Fontana Dam and the park.

Hike 27

Solitude, Far up the Creek

August 29
Trails: Deep Creek, Fork Ridge
Trailhead weather conditions: 64 degrees, clear, calm
Round-trip miles hiked: 12.8

I've hiked the lower part of the fourteen-mile-long Deep Creek Trail numerous times since the 1980s. It's been at least twenty-five years, however, since I've traversed its upper reaches near the stream's headwaters and the Smokies' crest. But this is the hiking plan today, a plan that means I'll start at the path's northern trailhead near Newfound Gap and descend steeply into the Deep Creek drainage, which lies essentially in the heart of the park. After a few miles, I intend to take a right onto Fork Ridge Trail, which after crossing the creek climbs steadily for about five miles before reaching Clingmans Dome Road near Mount Collins. The latter trail, which doubles as a section of North Carolina's Mountains-to-Sea Trail, courses above a nearly impossible-to-reach natural feature that has gained a prominent place in Cherokee and Smokies lore.

As I start down the trail, I think about the contrast between these high-altitude environs—starting at roughly forty-eight hundred feet—and the Deep Creek tubing run about three thousand feet lower, just inside the park boundary near Bryson City. That low-elevation section of the creek, a few miles above its confluence with the Tuckasegee River, is usually teeming with tubists during the summer. Up here, however, the solitude and rugged terrain give no hint of the fact that far downstream is a mile-long stretch of splashy tubing in Deep Creek's beautiful, bracing waters.

A pleasantly cool morning has the feel of fall as I make my usual brief stop at the Oconaluftee Visitor Center, about twenty minutes from the trailhead. Although July and August have been unusually warm and wet across much of the Smokies, I confess to having mixed feelings about the approaching autumn. Not that fall isn't typically a wonderful season in the mountains. It's what follows that I'm not necessarily thrilled about—cold, dark, windy, and often icy winter. I've become less and less enamored of it as I've grown older. The waning days of summer? I'll cling to them.

After driving more than ten miles farther up Newfound Gap Road, I arrive at the trailhead for Deep Creek Trail. The small parking area is wide open on a quiet Monday in the park. This is clearly the calm before the Labor Day weekend storm of visitors later in the week. I look down into the lengthy Deep Creek Valley and enjoy the islands in the clouds: mountain peaks rising above the fogbound lower elevations. With lofty Noland Divide soaring to the right, it's a lovely view from here, marred only by several dead hemlock trees not far below the parking area.

As I head down into a deep, dark forest, a few switchbacks make the sharp initial descent from the trailhead much easier than it would be otherwise. There's no sign or sound of a creek or even a tributary at the outset, but within a mile the trail crosses a headwaters branch and soon Deep Creek itself emerges in the steep terrain. With the sun now emerging over the ridge, dappled sunlight brightens the forest as the trail starts to level. I stop for a drink of water and promptly receive a scolding from a noisy red squirrel—it's not called a mountain boomer for nothing.

Soon I encounter a challenge: a merger of the trail and creek with the path's continuation on land not immediately apparent, partly because of large fallen trees across the stream. I walk on rocks into shallow water, and then work my way through the blowdowns. After negotiating the latter, I spot the trail's land route to the left and gladly step onto it. From here, my boots stay mostly dry until I swap Deep Creek Trail for Fork Ridge Trail in fewer than three miles.

Back on dry land, the trail soon rises well above a bolder Deep Creek. I enjoy some fine views of the rushing creek, dotted with churning white-water cascades. In an area where the trail is narrow, overgrown, and wet—apparently it rained here the previous day—I spot a lone goldenrod, previewing the approaching season. The trail drops back to creek level, where Deep Creek is now roaring as it flows through a green gorge the stream has carved over the eons.

About four miles from the road, Deep Creek Trail arrives at the junction with Fork Ridge Trail, just above the descriptively named Poke Patch backcountry campsite. From the looks of it, the basically flat, open camping area receives plenty of use, and perhaps some abuse. No way that pokeweed or anything else could now grow in the large, blackened area around the massive rock fire ring in the middle of the camp; a *de facto* scorched-earth policy seems to be in effect here. But nearby are a couple of nice sitting logs, one of which I land on for an early lunch in the sun.

After lunch, I'm faced with a backcountry conundrum: how to safely cross Deep Creek in order to hike up Fork Ridge—or whether to cross it at all and instead continue down Deep Creek Trail. Although the Mountains-to-Sea Trail piggybacks on Fork Ridge Trail up to Clingmans Dome Road, there's no footbridge for hikers to use in order to get across this twenty-five-foot crossing of Deep Creek. I walk a short distance up and down the creek looking for a safe, dry passage, but to no avail. Although water levels don't seem unusually high for a late-August day, I'll need to take a few steps in calf-deep water in order to ford the stream, so that's what I decide to do. With the help of a hiking pole, I make it across without incident, but my boots will be wet for the rest of the outing because removing them to cross did not seem a wise choice considering the creek's rocky streambed.

The next challenge is a steep climb on a mostly narrow, leaning trail to nearby Deep Creek Gap, located at an elevation more than two hundred feet higher than the creek. At the gap, I hear the roar of Deep Creek's Left Fork, joining that of the main stem. Here, the two streams are only about one-third mile apart, before eventually meeting a few miles downstream. Above the gap, the hiking becomes relatively easy on a moderate grade through a dry pine-oak forest. At a slight gap, looking north through the foliage, I spot what I think is fifty-eight-hundred-foot Mount Mingus, rising to the northwest of Newfound Gap.

As I continue up Fork Ridge, the trail becomes overgrown and slightly washed out in a few places. Flying away in a small cove is a ruffed grouse, surprisingly the first one I've actually seen—and not just heard—in the Smokies all year. Next to the trail is a lone red spruce, a sure sign that the trail has now climbed above four thousand feet. Soon I hear what I think is the faint sound of a little-seen, but well-chronicled, tributary of Deep Creek's Left Fork: Keg Drive Branch.

During the merciless Trail of Tears, Cherokee fugitive Tsali temporarily eluded capture by federal troops by reputedly hiding beneath a large rock overhang along Keg Drive Branch, in the rough terrain below the present-day Fork Ridge Trail. (Although stories differ on the origin of the branch's name, it's probably safe to say that the Left Fork tributary didn't get its name from a fraternity keg party.) Because it's no easier to reach the remote location of Tsali's hideout today than it was in 1838, I'm perfectly content remaining on the safe, maintained trail above it.

About halfway up the five-mile Left Fork Trail, I decide it's time to turn back because this point is nearly 6½ miles from the Deep Creek trailhead on Newfound Gap Road and a round-trip of about thirteen miles seems enough for today. At a couple of breaks in the trees, I have fine views of nearby Noland Divide as I hike back toward Deep Creek. Below Deep Creek Gap, I slide slightly off the steep, narrow trail at one point, but remain upright and unscathed. I arrive at the creek and steel myself to get wet again, but it's really no big deal as my boots are still wet from the first crossing anyway. After fording the stream this second time, I cool off further by splashing my face with creek water.

It's muggy and buggy most of the way back up Deep Creek Trail—no, summer hasn't vanished—and soon I trade the roar of the creek for the roar of motorcycles on Newfound Gap Road, still high above the trail. I also hear a few katydids in the dense forest and the *cluck-cluck-cluck* of a wild turkey, but I never do spot the bird. I arrive at the car without having seen anyone on the entire trip, in great contrast to the summertime throngs on the lower section of one of the Smokies' loveliest streams.

Hike 28

Stiff Climb to Sterling

September 7
Trails: Baxter Creek, Mount Sterling, Mount Sterling Ridge, Swallow Fork, Big Creek
Trailhead weather conditions: 63 degrees, clear, calm
Round-trip miles hiked: 17.1

Describing the weather in the Great Smoky Mountains as unpredictable is not engaging in hyperbole. Most any time of year, weather shifts in the Smokies can be sudden and dramatic. Although the weather often differs slightly from cove to cove, typically the major disparities owe to fast moving fronts, localized summer storms, or elevation differences. Regarding the latter, Exhibit A in the Smokies may be Baxter Creek Trail, a demanding 6¼-mile path from Big Creek to the summit of Mount Sterling. With an elevation gain of more than forty-one hundred feet, the trail can bring substantial variations in the elements during any season. But the changes also can be hazardous on occasion. I've experienced weather conditions atop the 5,842-foot-high Mount Sterling that were crazily different from those at the 1,700-foot-elevation Big Creek.

Mindful of that history, today I plan another trip to Mount Sterling, site of what is reputedly the highest-elevation fire tower in the eastern United States. The Mount Sterling tower rises about nine hundred feet higher than the next highest tower still standing in the Smokies. As I recall from previous visits, the tower is similar to the one on Shuckstack that I visited in August. It is a steel structure about sixty feet tall that also was constructed in the mid-1930s. But the Sterling tower was built by the Civilian Conservation Corps, rather than the Public Works

Administration. Not surprisingly, the views from the tower are exceptional when it's not bathed in clouds at its lofty elevation. As for today's weather, the forecast calls for warm, sunny conditions with basically no chance of rain. We'll see how that plays out, as Mount Sterling often seems to have a mind of its own when it comes to the elements. In any case, I'm determined not to be defeated by the weather today, even if I have no control over it.

In terms of both climate and vegetation, the hike up Baxter Creek Trail from Big Creek to Mount Sterling is somewhat akin to traveling from North Georgia to Central Maine, as if hiking the entire twenty-two-hundred-mile Appalachian Trail. At a good pace, in about three hours, I hike from a low-elevation Southern Appalachian ecosytem to a boreal zone dominated by red spruce and Fraser fir. (Fortunately, the balsam woolly adelgid, first discovered in the Smokies on Mount Sterling more than a half-century ago, doesn't attack red spruce as it does Fraser fir.) Along the way, I see some huge hardwoods that managed to escape being logged. The forest diversity really is a remarkable thing to experience on a single trail barely more than six miles long.

Only four cars are parked at the parking area for the trailhead and Big Creek picnic ground upon my arrival about 8:30 A.M.—fewer cars than were here exactly seven months ago in February on my last trip to Big Creek. But it is a weekday just after the Labor Day rush, so I'm not too surprised by the low number of cars, all of which probably belong to backpackers at this time of day. I smell a bit of wood smoke, confirmation that people are camping at the nearby developed campground. Although it's a seasonally cool morning, by the time I

return in late afternoon, the temperature at this elevation will be well into the eighties.

A sturdy steel bridge spanning rocky, roiling Big Creek marks the start of the formidable Baxter Creek Trail and the major elevation gain I have ahead of me. The bridge also is the northern terminus of the three-hundred-mile Benton MacKaye Trail, which begins in North Georgia and reaches North Carolina by way of southeast Tennessee. The lengthy path piggybacks Baxter Creek Trail for an especially scenic and diverse six-mile finale after crossing Mount Sterling—the highest point of the entire three hundred miles.

As I hike through a mostly flat, open area near the trailhead, I encounter a few blowdowns across the trail. Although they're easy to negotiate with the level terrain, they initially give the trail the feel of a path that hasn't been maintained for a while. Between the trail and Big Creek are the remains of a large chimney formerly attached to a lodge built during the area's logging days. Those days certainly left a lasting imprint on the Big Creek watershed.

In about a half hour, there's an easy rock-hop crossing of Baxter Creek, a stream that curiously makes only a cameo along the trail that bears its name. Soon, I see a cluster of white wood asters along the trail, just before an opening in the forest yields a fine view across the Pigeon River Gorge, which I drove through earlier to reach the park. I cross a branch of Baxter Creek, and, except for a seep or two, I will see no more water on the trail—it's dry all the way to the top.

In short order, I meet a total of five backpackers, in three bursts, who are hiking out after camping overnight at the Mount Sterling backcountry site—the highest camp in the park without a trail shelter. A solo young woman from Michigan, nearing the end of her first trip to the Smokies, relates that she climbed the Mount Sterling tower to watch the sun rise. "I'm in awe of how beautiful everything is," she gushes. Her view of the Smokies sharply contrasts with Bill Bryson's sour review in his book about hiking part of the Appalachian Trail.

The ascent, on a good grade, now becomes mostly unrelenting, as one might expect with an elevation gain exceeding four thousand feet in just over six miles. A pileated woodpecker makes its shrieking presence felt, if not seen, soon followed by the *rat-a-tat* of a red squirrel. Next, there are human sounds from a garrulous group headed down the trail. They are apparently the final wave of backpackers who pulled in at Mount Sterling campsite the previous day.

Finally, after a long steady climb, the trail reaches a switchback with a sign that directs descending hikers to take a sharp left in order to bypass the abandoned Big Branch Trail. I'm guessing that this trail, which also began at Big Creek, is one reason Baxter Creek Trail acquired its name from a creek it barely meets. That, along with the fact that two trails carry the Sterling name on the far side of Mount Sterling. Below this bend of Baxter Creek Trail is a short section of riprap, surely the handiwork of the CCC. At this switchback, the path finally begins climbing the spine of Mount Sterling Ridge. It becomes obvious in places that someone has recently cleared some thick undergrowth, making travel a bit easier than it was last time I was here.

The trail works its way up the ridge, entering an area where red spruce becomes more and more prevalent among the northern hardwood trees—a particularly pleasant sight after seeing many massive dead hemlocks that have succumbed to the hemlock woolly adelgid. Soon I reach a switchback, which gives a false sense that Mount Sterling's summit might be within range. In fact, the last time I hiked here with Karen, she asked hikers coming down if we were near the top and one replied, smugly, if not gleefully, "Ohhhhh no." But

yes, there's still some work to do before the trail finally plays out at the tower.

After another bend in the trail, I continue through an area that has the look of a temperate rain forest with its lush growth and carpet of spongy moss. I hear what I think may be a raven, rather than a crow at this high elevation, but I don't get even a glimpse of the bird through the thick foliage. Soon, a trail sign notes that water can be found seven hundred feet off the main path, via a side trail. At this point, Baxter Creek Trail begins a final steep assault of about one-third mile toward the summit of Mount Sterling.

There's not a soul in sight upon my arrival at the top just after noon. And the weather? It's mild and mostly sunny, in contrast to my last summertime trip to Mount Sterling when a fierce thunderstorm produced a cold, driving rain that was nearly ideal for also producing hypothermia. And today is in greater contrast still to a November volunteer outing several years ago, when not only the tower but also the summit itself featured a thin, treacherous glaze of ice. Ice skates would have been handy . . . if I had known how to ice skate.

Although a power-line swath allows views looking east, Sterling's verdant crown of red spruce requires a climb up the fire tower in order to see the panorama of soft, green mountains unfold. So up I go—six flights and nearly eighty steps—to reach the top of the tower. (*Footnote*: Duke Energy is seeking approval to install a solar-panel array to replace the current overhead line that powers park communications equipment atop the mountain. Renewable-energy benefits notwithstanding, the thirty-panel micro-grid certainly stands to alter the character of the Sterling summit, just as the tower did in the 1930s.)

As with Shuckstack on the opposite end of the park, the 360-degree views are stunning. With binoculars, I spot the low-slung, octagonal lookout tower on nearby Mount Cammerer, which I plan to visit in October. Prominent to the northwest is the Smokies' second highest peak, Mount Guyot. But my favorite view is to the southwest, where I see the hulking, 6,155-foot Big Cataloochee Mountain, rising broadly amid a sea of green near the junction of Mount Sterling Ridge and Balsam Mountain. Below me, among the lovely red spruce, I see a couple of mountain ash with their reddish-orange berries adding high-elevation color in September. It's an exceptional perch, just above fifty-nine hundred feet in elevation if one tacks on the tower's sixty-foot height.

After lunch, I gingerly descend the tower and decide to poke around the Mount Sterling backcountry campsite, which had plenty of business overnight. At a secluded site, I spot a blackened kitchen pot that has perhaps been left intentionally for community use. I then make a more significant decision: to continue hiking away from the Big Creek trailhead, traveling the Mount Sterling, Mount Sterling Ridge, Swallow Fork, and Big Creek Trails back to my car. The loop route will add nearly five miles to my trip, but because I'm departing the campsite about one o'clock I should have plenty of time to close the loop before dark.

I set out on Mount Sterling Trail, passing hitching posts on my left. (By forsaking a return on Baxter Creek Trail, I hike on horse trails the rest of the day.) It's only about a half-mile to the junction with Mount Sterling Ridge Trail, where I bear right toward Pretty Hollow Gap and Swallow Fork Trail. Just before starting a brief ascent of a small knob, I inadvertently flush several wild turkeys to the left of the path. Soon, I arrive at the gap, where three backpackers have pulled in after climbing from Big Creek. I turn right on Swallow Fork Trail and begin a steady descent, enjoying a brief view through an opening to my left of Low Gap on the Appalachian Trail. The character of the trail changes at the first switchback, when the path turns away from Mount Sterling Ridge and begins dipping deeper into the Swallow Fork drainage. About halfway down, near a rock-hop creek crossing, I meet another solo backpacker. The lanky young man says he began visiting the Smokies with his parents when he was six years old, but has just now started to enjoy the adventures of backpacking. After crossing Swallow Fork on a foot log less than a half hour later, I'm within a mile of Big Creek Trail, which will lead me back to the car in another five miles or so.

In addition to foliage and undergrowth that were absent along the creek seven months ago, I find the Big Creek route much drier than it was in early February. For example, a concrete ford that I waded through then is now desert dry. And Mouse Creek Falls, which in the winter came crashing off the ridge into Big Creek about two miles from the trailhead, today is just a trickle by comparison. But Midnight Hole, the popular swimming spot a bit farther downstream, still seems plenty deep enough for a cooling plunge.

Soon, I'm back at the parking area, after being on the trail from roughly nine to five on another good day's work (?) in the Smokies' backcountry. Although I typically savor solitude on my outings as a way to clear the clutter from my head, today I especially enjoyed the brief encounters I had with several backpackers—mostly twenty-somethings who seemed glad to engage in conversation with a graybeard day hiker. Perhaps all of them will be able to enjoy the fresh air and natural beauty of Great Smoky Mountains National Park well into its second century, long after I've bowed out.

Hike 29

Summer's Last Stand

September 21
Trails: Deep Creek, Indian
Creek, Deeplow Gap,
Thomas Divide, Newton
Bald, Sunkota Ridge,
Loop
*Trailhead weather
conditions:* 57 degrees,
clear, calm
Round-trip miles hiked: 20.5

On this final official day of summer, I plan to make what may also be my final volunteer trip of the year, up to the Newton Bald backcountry campsite I've maintained for several years. But this excursion will require much more hiking than this year's three previous volunteer trips, because I've decided to start from Deep Creek for a loop of about twenty miles on all or part of seven different trails. OK, call me crazy. Although I hiked this lengthy route several years ago, before I turned sixty, no doubt it's going to pose a challenge for me at age sixty-four. Having plenty of food and, especially, water is essential, as I'll likely be in the woods for about ten hours, including campsite cleanup time.

Speaking of water, I've decided to revisit the camp today in part because the Smokies' backcountry office has asked about water flow at the usually reliable spring near the site. It's never come close to running dry in all the years I've worked the campsite, but the past month or so was exceptionally dry in Asheville and the same may be true for the Newton Bald area, which I've not visited since early July. In any event, I'll find out the spring's status after several hours of climbing to about five thousand feet, just off what likely will be a thirsty Thomas Divide considering this year's rainfall deficit.

The early-morning fog enveloping Bryson City is dissipating as I drive up the Deep Creek Valley toward the park boundary. The vanishing fog yields beautiful views of high mountains to the north inside the park. It's shaping up as a fine day to be in the woods. Not surprisingly, upon entering the park I find the Deep Creek picnic ground and trailhead parking area dramatically quieter than they were on my last visit over the Memorial Day weekend, when parking anywhere was scarce at best. The creek itself is quieter, too, as water levels are running low after a mostly dry summer; tubing in the creek today would not be easy. I spot a waning moon above the spacious parking lot as I lace up my boots and prepare for my longest hike of the year.

In a few minutes, I find lovely Tom Branch Falls is relatively puny today as it spills off the ridge. Accessible as the falls are, it's unusual not to see anyone else admiring them, as is the case this morning. The same is true of Indian Creek Falls, after I take a right onto Indian Creek Trail about three-fourths of a mile from the trailhead. Proceeding up the trail, I finally do meet three hikers and then a cyclist in the dark, humid valley pinched by Sunkota Ridge and Thomas Divide. Lumbering across the trail much farther up, near the Deeplow Gap Trail junction, is a black bear—the only mammal I'll see for several hours. I stop at the junction for a snack and a drink of water, for I'm about to begin some serious climbing to Deeplow Gap itself. The lower part of Deeplow Gap Trail is also rocky and wet. Yes, the easy roadbed hiking is over.

On my right in less than a half-mile, I pass Georges Branch backcountry campsite, which I maintained for a couple of years less than a decade ago. Although spaces with open, level spots for tents are scarce here, it's a nice camp with a typically reliable water source. I continue up the trail, crossing several tributaries of Georges Branch, before encountering an area of dead hemlocks, in contrast to some healthy ones I saw on Indian Creek. After the trail makes a switchback to the right, the tread is smoother and drier as it climbs on a good grade toward Deeplow Gap, the lowest point on the upper ten miles of the lengthy, towering Thomas Divide. At the gap, the silence is slightly broken by distant traffic, likely from Great Smoky Mountains Expressway.

After the stiff climb from Indian Creek, it seems as if Deeplow Gap should be much higher than its elevation of 3,715 feet. But it soon becomes obvious that the altitude is less than four thousand feet, as the Thomas Divide Trail I take north from the gap climbs steeply for the next couple of miles to achieve an elevation of nearly five thousand feet. Along the way, acorns are plentiful in places underfoot, perhaps an indication that mast will be abundant this year. (Park wildlife biologists confirm about a week later that there is indeed a bumper crop of hard mast and mountain-ash berries this year—good news for a variety of wildlife.) About a mile after the trail finally levels, I reach a junction for not only Newton Bald Trail, but also for the Mountains-to-Sea and Benton MacKaye Trails that tag along to the Newton Bald backcountry campsite and beyond. Although the trail sign at the junction notes the distance to the camp as being two-tenths mile, it's no more than one hundred yards on a path, lined by a welcoming party of goldenrods on this golden September day.

Upon arriving at the campsite—a noisy arrival initially as wild turkeys are clucking away on either side of the camp—I hang my pack on one of the food-cable hooks. The next task is to walk down a steep side trail in order to check the usually reliable spring. Although I find it to be partially clogged by debris and moss, the spring still has a good flow despite the recent dry weather. I clean it and marvel at the steady flow gurgling out of the ground near the crest of a dry high-elevation ridge. Surely, it must be one of the most dependable springs in the Smokies.

The campsite area is beautiful and peaceful as I pick up trash, break down a couple of large rock fire rings, and scatter fireplace ashes in the surrounding woods. After finishing my work, I retrieve my pack and eat a late lunch. I'm loath to leave this lovely camp, but I still have more than eleven miles to hike on my marathon loop, and the days have grown noticeably shorter now that the autumnal equinox is at hand.

I head north for less than a half-mile on Thomas Divide Trail before turning left onto Sunkota Ridge, which I follow for its entire length of about nine miles. Its upper five miles, constructed by the Civilian Conservation Corps, provide a pleasant, if unspectacular, woodland journey. I'm always puzzled, and a bit amused, by first-time park visitors who express disappointment that trails in the Smokies don't provide a thrilling vista every minute; the remarkable variety of trees and plants would seem to be enjoyable enough. After a couple of miles, in a small gap at about four thousand feet in elevation, there's a pleasant breeze and a nice view through the trees of the mighty Smokies' crest. Deep Creek flows far below.

As I continue descending toward Martins Gap, I enter a pine/oak forest, where fallen pine needles provide soft footing on the well-graded trail. Near the gap, soaring Noland Divide becomes visible through the trees to the right. I stop to rest at the gap, since I have more climbing to do: a four-hundred-foot ascent to an elevation exceeding thirty-eight hundred feet along Sunkota Ridge. From that point to a junction with Deep Creek Loop Trail, it's almost all downhill.

After turning right onto Loop Trail, I'm pleasantly surprised to find that extensive trail work has been done to improve what had been a badly rutted path in places. The improvements include water bars and a couple of raised sections or trail turnpikes. The additions make the walk down to Deep Creek much more enjoyable than it was the last time I was here. As I hang a left onto Deep Creek Trail for the final 1¾ miles of my own ambitious loop, I begin to see mammals—Homo sapiens—again, including a middle-aged couple, who ask how to find the third waterfall (Juney Whank) of Deep Creek's popular three-waterfalls hike.

Soon I'm back at the parking area, fatigued but gratified that I have pulled off a twenty-mile day hike. If my math is correct, I've now piled up more than three hundred trail miles in the Smokies this year, on my way to at least four hundred if everything goes according to plan. Now it's time for a fourth season of hiking, and the most colorful one in the Smokies, courtesy of fall foliage. So long, summer of '16—a scorcher for the most part, but one that has yielded many enjoyable, rain-free hikes.

Hike 30

Thunderhead—the Mountain

September 28
Trails: Lead Cove, Bote
 Mountain, Appalachian,
 Eagle Creek
Trailhead weather
 conditions: 61 degrees,
 clear, calm
Round-trip miles hiked: 13.5

People's names aside, some of the place names along the Appalachian Trail in the Smokies are much more descriptive and original than others; Shuckstack, The Sawteeth, and of course, Charlies Bunion quickly come to mind. The name of today's destination, Thunderhead Mountain, is in that select group, too. At an altitude of 5,527 feet, Thunderhead is also notable as the final peak in the Smokies going south on the AT that attains an elevation above fifty-five hundred feet. But its southwestern rampart, the likewise descriptively named Rocky Top, actually provides the sweeping views, despite being nearly one hundred feet lower. I aim for both spots today, on what shapes up as a beautiful late-September day.

Although I previously hiked to Thunderhead nearly three decades ago, today I'm traveling a slightly different route to get there. I'll still pick up the Appalachian Trail at Spence Field southwest of Thunderhead, but I'll go by way of Lead Cove Trail to Bote Mountain Trail. The out-and-back hike of about thirteen miles will bring me up to fifty for the month, after two even lengthier hikes. I've also covered all or part of fifty different trails this year. With three more months of hiking, it now looks as if I'll blow past sixty trails in 2016 on my way to four-hundred-plus miles and more than one million steps. But I'm not there yet.

The main reason I've forsaken the enticing Thunderhead for so long is the driving time required and the frequent heavy traffic encountered to get within striking distance by foot. From my house in Asheville, it's well over two hours by car to reach the trailheads in Tennessee that provide reasonable day hikes to Thunderhead. I'm feeling some urgency to return, because vehicles headed to Cades Cove during the park's frenzied fall-color season will likely jam Laurel Creek Road, where the Lead Cove trailhead is located. The trails to Thunderhead won't exactly be deserted, either.

Yes, I really thought I might find the park roads leading to Lead Cove trailhead lightly traveled early on a weekday in September. Not so—not on the Tennessee side, at least. Traffic quickly begins to thicken once I clear the state line at Newfound Gap. And several miles farther down Newfound Gap Road, the large parking area for the heavily used Chimney Tops Trail is filling up fast. Fortunately, about an hour later, I find parking spaces at my chosen trailhead still available on either side of Laurel Creek Road.

Actually, I have a choice of trails from the parking area this morning. On the west side of the road, I can access Turkeypen Ridge and Crib Gap Trails; on the east, Finley Cane and Lead Cove. I opt for Lead Cove, as it provides the shortest route to the AT—about 4¾ miles, with a hefty elevation gain of more than three thousand feet.

I set out just past 10:00 A.M. in a cool, damp forest and find the trail has a slightly scoured look; apparently the path had rainfall runoff earlier this week. Soon, after an easy rock-hop crossing of Laurel Cove Creek, I begin climbing in earnest; the trail ascends from about eighteen hundred to three thousand feet in only about 1¾

miles. I have long since lost the din of road traffic by the time I reach an opening in the forest that yields a nice view of nearby Scott Mountain. In a few more minutes, I arrive at Sandy Gap, formerly the name of the trail I've been on to this point. The gap is open and sunny, as Bote Mountain Trail—a former roadbed—runs through here. To my left is a wide, flat section of the old road, but to my right (where I'm headed) the trail quickly becomes steep and rocky. Through the pines and hardwoods I can see part of the imposing Smokies' crest that I'll meet in slightly more than an hour. There's also some early fall color at the gap, courtesy of dogwood foliage. It's a pleasant spot for a snack and drink of water after the first leg of my hike.

By the way, the place name *Bote* is likely a corruption of "vote," which supposedly originated from the road's construction workers—Cherokee Indians and/or perhaps an immigrant—who in their pronunciation "boted" in the 1830s for this particular route to the Smokies' crest. Today, I'm "boting" with my feet to follow the Bote Mountain Trail for about three miles to the Appalachian Trail, gaining nearly two thousand additional feet in elevation in the process.

Soon, I start my climb on a mostly wide course, thanks to the old roadbed. Shortly before arriving at a junction with Anthony Creek Trail, I see a sizable scattering of feathers in the middle of the trail; a large bird of some sort has lost a battle here. Once I reach the trail junction, I pick up the same route I used in 1987 to reach Thunderhead, though I have absolutely no recollection of the route on its climb to the AT. A solo backpacker scurrying down the trail announces in passing that he's "feeling the cold coming on, so I'm headed out west to hike the Pacific Crest Trail." Ah, to be young and apparently unencumbered by commitments.

In a few minutes, I walk through a former road turnaround and continue on Bote Mountain Trail. The trail is so badly eroded in places that it basically becomes a deep, steep-banked trough. The path climbs steadily in a mostly straight, due-south direction before a switchback heralds the final approach to the AT junction at Spence Field, a formerly prodigious grassy bald that woody and herbaceous plants are overtaking. At the junction, I'm in a northern hardwood forest at an elevation of about forty-nine hundred feet, or slightly more than six hundred feet lower than the Thunderhead summit. I'm climbing more than that from here, however, because the AT rises and falls as it works its way toward the mountain.

About one-third mile east (north on the AT) of the Bote Mountain Trail junction, I reach another junction, this one with the Jenkins Ridge Trail, which descends several miles to the Lakeshore Trail meandering near Fontana Lake. A benchmark on a boulder notes that the elevation here is still less than 5,000 feet—4,950, to be exact. From here, I begin a stiff climb, with one short descent, toward Rocky Top. At one point en route I see a battalion of berry-laden mountain ash, further evidence that wildlife should have plenty to eat this fall. I meet a solo hiker who tells me to "say hi to the gal at Rocky Top," but upon my arrival, there is no gal—or guy—at Rocky Top. However, almost immediately after I drop my pack and begin eating a late lunch, three day hikers arrive from the opposite direction, giving me impetus to press on to finish the remaining three-fourths mile to Thunderhead. Although the Thunderhead summit is overgrown, a few stacked rocks provide a vantage point for nice views looking south into North Carolina. A wooden sign that once stood here is gone, but a benchmark notes the elevation of 5,527 feet.

Working back toward Rocky Top, I cross a fine open lookout just below fifty-five hundred feet that apparently lacks an official name—call it Thunder Rock?—before I arrive again at what is now a hiker-free Rocky Top. I

have this open, rocky perch to myself for a while, and some perch it is on a cloudless September afternoon. The vistas in all directions are remarkable—of Clingmans Dome and Mount Le Conte, of Cades Cove, of Gregory Bald, of my old friend Shuckstack and its little brother Little Shuckstack, of the Eagle Creek watershed and a piece of Fontana Lake, of nearby Welch Ridge and its high point, the aptly named High Rocks. Outside the park, distant mountain ranges in North Carolina such as the Nantahalas, Cowees, and Plott Balsams are clearly visible. It's a truly magnificent spot on the western end of the park. Rocky Top is also the inspiration for the eponymous tune that at some point overtook, if unofficially, "Down the Field" as the Tennessee Volunteers' fight song. Although the catchy tune proclaims that Rocky Top will "always be home sweet home to me," surely this high-elevation outcrop has never been home to any human for any period of time. Lyrical license, I suppose.

After a while, I hear voices of hikers headed toward the lookout, so I proceed to pack up. I meet three cheerful young men from nearby Knoxville fewer than one hundred yards down the trail from Rocky Top and relate that they are about to enjoy a view-fest. Heading down to the Jenkins Ridge Trail junction, I see swards of mountain oat grass on either side of the trail. At a grassy opening to my left, I savor one last distant view of Fontana Lake beyond the far end of the Eagle Creek watershed.

Back at the Bote Mountain Trail junction, I decide to take a short side trip to Eagle Creek Trail, which leads to the Spence Field trail shelter about one-fourth mile away. (Karen and I backpacked the lower, stream-fording section of Eagle Creek Trail in 1985.) I'm glad I make this decision, as the nearly spotless shelter is located in a lovely, quiet spot off the busy AT. I decide to check the nearby water source and discover that, despite the generally dry weather, there's a low, but steady, flow from a well-placed pipe. I will report this to the backcountry office the next day, just in case staff or volunteers haven't recently checked the source.

After a few minutes, I leave the shelter area and head back to Bote Mountain Trail. On the way down, at the Anthony Creek Trail junction, I meet a solo backpacker who is aiming for the Spence Field shelter. He's carrying a large, half-empty plastic bottle of soda but says he forgot his water bottles. Perhaps he will do OK by simply refilling the soda bottle with filtered water from the pipe near the shelter.

Farther still down the trail, I stop again briefly at Sandy Gap, enjoying one last splash of September sunshine, before turning left onto Lead Cove Trail. Although there's plenty of remaining daylight, I proceed quickly down the trail, knowing that I will be dealing with heavy vehicle traffic at least as far as Newfound Gap. And sure enough, while I regroup at the trailhead, a steady stream of cars whizzes past me in either direction on Laurel Creek Road. I have to wonder what traffic will be like in October, especially on weekends, if it is this thick on a September weekday. Are we loving the Smokies into submission?

Hike 31

Last of the Lookout Towers

October 5
Trails: Chestnut Branch,
   Appalachian, Mount
   Cammerer
*Trailhead weather
   conditions:* 60 degrees,
   clear, calm
Round-trip miles hiked: 12.0

Today I aim to complete the final trip of this year's tower trilogy that began with Shuckstack and Mount Sterling: a hike to craggy Mount Cammerer, a five-thousand-foot mountain, crowned by a distinctive stone octagonal lookout also no longer used as a fire tower. Built in the late 1930s by the Civilian Conservation Corps, the tower is the Smokies' northeastern sentinel, before the soaring Smokies' crest falls off sharply toward the Pigeon River and its dramatic gorge. Although the low-slung Mount Cammerer lookout doesn't rise nearly as high as the sixty-foot-tall towers on Shuckstack and Mount Sterling, the views it offers are no less stunning. (A fourth tower still standing in the Smokies atop Cove Mountain, along the park boundary in Tennessee, is off-limits to hikers because it's now used to monitor air quality.)

The hike to Mount Cammerer—once known variously as White Rock, Sharp Top, or Old Mother—is steeper and longer from the Big Creek section of the park than it is from the Cosby section in Tennessee. But Karen and I decide to take the route from Big Creek, on the North Carolina side, partly because it's easier for us to reach by car. The total elevation gain of thirty-three hundred feet begins with a significant climb on the two-mile Chestnut Branch Trail, followed by a steady ascent of about 3⅓ miles on the Appalachian Trail and an up-and-down course on the short Mount Cammerer spur trail. It's a stern test, but one that has a big payoff at the end.

The large parking area next to the Big Creek ranger station has plenty of available spaces upon our arrival shortly before 9:30 A.M. It's another clear, cool morning, an ideal start to what will prove to be a gorgeous Indian summer day. The trailhead for Chestnut Branch Trail, which initially follows an old logging road, is just a few steps away. Near its start are a horse barrier, allowing a narrow trail access for hikers only, and what looks like an old cistern on the left. Autumn sunlight pours through the mostly second-growth forest as the trail rises steeply, before leveling off on an easy grade. After a half-mile or so, the path reaches an area where a Presbyterian mission school and church were built in 1920, several years before authorization of the park. Fall wildflowers—mostly asters and goldenrods, but also a few gentians—are spotted in a few places. To our left, Chestnut Branch tumbles toward a meeting with Big Creek near the trailhead.

After a mile or so, the trail courses to the right, away from Chestnut Branch, and begins a short, but steep, climb up the ridge to a switchback. The grade then eases before the path does a dance with a tributary of Chestnut Branch as we make our way toward the AT junction. We rest before the final ascent—an even steeper one until the trail terminates at an open area just below three thousand feet. The junction leaves us with a remaining elevation gain of about two thousand feet before we meet the Mount Cammerer spur in about 3⅓ miles. A long, hard pull awaits us.

As might be expected, the AT wastes no time in beginning the steady climb toward Mount Cammerer. We walk through a rhododendron tunnel, and then turn sharply right to travel a dry ridge. Soon, we meet a couple of backpackers coming down, the first of several we'll see on our way up and down the AT. About a mile above Chestnut Branch Trail, we arrive at another expansive junction where the Lower Mount Cammerer Trail terminates. That trail has zigzagged more than seven miles coming up from Cosby Campground on the Tennessee side. Here, we've reached the halfway point of our six-mile route to the Mount Cammerer Fire Tower.

Above the trail junction, soon after our lengthy climb resumes, we see a short side trail to the left, noted in an Appalachian Trail Data Book as a path to a spring. Although we don't check it out, I would guess it's running low, if at all, after several weeks of dry weather. A solo backpacker hurriedly heading south has a one-word reply when asked where he's headed: Georgia. We continue climbing, hiking through a boulder field as the trail ascends. At the second of two switchbacks—a point that brings us under the Mount Cammerer ridgeline—we enjoy a fine view across the Pigeon River Gorge toward Tennessee's Snowbird Mountain. But there's an even more dramatic vista farther up the trail, at a rock outcrop just past a sturdy rock wall. Soaring Mount Sterling is prominent from the outcrop, rising well above a nearer ridge separating the Chestnut Branch and Big Creek Valleys. We have a bite of lunch before beginning the final push of a mile or so to Mount Cammerer Trail.

At last, after the arduous climb, we arrive at the junction with the spur trail to the lookout. A benchmark notes the elevation here as 4,949 feet, or 21 feet higher than the fire tower's altitude out on the ridge, which drops off precipitously. As we hike toward the lookout, the spur starts to seem longer than the six-tenths mile indicated on the trail sign, but perhaps that's because the rugged course dips and climbs on a rocky path.

Soon after a hitching post where horses must be left, the fire tower comes into view, rising above the rock outcrops that also yield exceptional views of the surrounding mountains and Tennessee foothills. We encounter a dozen or so day hikers—all apparently from the Cosby section, for we haven't seen and won't see any of them on our Big Creek route. They have staked out various view spots on the rock outcrops near the tower. But that's still a smaller number than we've ever encountered on what has become an annual autumn trip for us.

Completed in 1939 after more than two years of construction, the Mount Cammerer Fire Tower (originally called White Rock Lookout Tower) looks nothing like the nearby Mount Sterling steel tower built by the CCC several years earlier. Located on a rocky precipice, the tower, with its squat design, mimics towers in the West. The CCC used native stone quarried just a few hundred feet away for the two-story structure, as well as native timbers for the steps, railings, observation room, and exterior walkway encircling the room. Restored in the mid-1990s, thanks to funding from Friends of Great Smoky Mountains National Park, the lookout remains a structure of great charm, despite the battering it takes from the elements on its lofty, exposed perch. A nearby interpretive sign notes that it is named for Arno Cammerer, National Park Service director from 1933 to 1940, who secured a critical commitment from John D. Rockefeller Jr. to donate $5 million to help establish the park.

As for the 360-degree views, they are extraordinary on this cloudless October afternoon. Prominent to the southwest, looming above the Smokies' crest, is the 6,621-foot Mount Guyot, second highest peak in the park. To the southeast, along Mount Sterling Ridge, is Mount Sterling itself at an elevation of 5,842 feet. Outside the park, among the Tennessee foothills to the north and northwest, the Pigeon River and Eng-lish Mountain are easily visible. It's truly a feast of vistas among Cammerer's crags, shrubs, and red spruce. As we walk back toward the AT, we're compelled to claim one last vantage point for a few minutes, atop a broad rock outcrop that drops off dramatically to the north. Even if these were the only views from Mount Cammerer, they would be well worth the strenuous hike.

We resume walking and arrive at the AT junction in about fifteen minutes. From here, we hike steadily downhill for nearly 5½ miles. One guidebook writer described the trip down the AT to Chestnut Branch Trail and then to Davenport Gap as an ordeal. But the only thing close to an ordeal we've ever experienced hiking down was a timber rattlesnake that stubbornly refused to leave the middle of a narrow section of trail. The rattler finally yielded its place in the warm October sun soon after a group of horseback riders arrived. The long AT descent does feature hundreds of short logs placed across the trail that require stepping down, giving slight jolts to the feet and knees. Still, the route's grade is mostly moderate, if often rocky. On the way down today, we encounter several backpackers headed for Cosby Knob shelter, situated about three miles beyond the Mount Cammerer spur.

At the junction with Chestnut Branch Trail, we regroup for a few minutes before starting the steep descent toward the branch. As usual, we have this trail to ourselves all the way back to the parking area. It's been another beautiful dry day in the Smokies, even as menacing Hurricane Matthew churns in the Atlantic. The destructive storm will have one beneficial effect—light-to-moderate rainfall from its outer bands will fall over parts of the Smokies and other parched areas within the next couple of days. But rain that falls in the mountains and piedmont comes at a heavy cost for southeastern coastal areas.

Hike 32

As Rugged and Remote as It Gets

October 10
Trails: Beech Gap (West), Hyatt Ridge, Enloe Creek
Trailhead weather conditions: 45 degrees, sunny, calm
Round-trip miles hiked: 11.6

In his book *Walking with Spring*, a wonderful personal account of the first Appalachian Trail "thru-hike" in 1948, Earl Shaffer quotes a North Georgia woman who describes Blood Mountain as "too wild lonesome up thar." Her colorful observation is not a bad way to depict the Smokies' Raven Fork section, surely the wildest and most rugged part of the park. One of its place names, for example, is the aptly named Breakneck Ridge, traversed by what is now an abandoned, badly overgrown trail that I'm not about to take on at my age. Raven Fork itself stands out among the park's primary streams because it does not have a roadbed or maintained trail paralleling it at least part of the way; the terrain is too rough. The Raven Fork drainage is an exceptionally beautiful place to visit on a blue-sky October day. Today I plan to explore part of its lower portion on a loop hike via three trails and a gravel road that allows vehicle access to the general area. Although there won't be any distant 360-degree views, as with some recent outings, I do expect to see some striking wilderness scenery.

On Columbus Day, as I drive past Cherokee Central School (K-12), I can't help but wonder how the arrival of

Columbus, which proved fateful for this continent's native peoples, is discussed in classrooms. In any case, I drive on the Cherokee Indian Reservation for several more miles on Big Cove Road, before turning right onto Straight Fork Road to reach the park boundary, just past the Tribal Trout Hatchery. It's a prototype October morning in the Smokies: cool, clear, dew-drenched, though with only a few pockets of fog. Once again, I could not have better conditions for a lengthy hike, in great contrast to the disastrous flooding that is continuing in eastern North Carolina. The drought we're experiencing in the mountains is trivial by comparison. (Alas, that will change in a few weeks.)

Not surprisingly, no vehicles are present upon my arrival at the large parking area—big enough to also accommodate several horse trailers—for the Hyatt Ridge trailhead about 2½ miles inside the park boundary. I meet one car on its way out of the park on the narrow gravel road, but otherwise I see no other signs of civilization inside the park. It's a typically quiet weekday in this remote part of the Smokies. In fact, the only person I see while hiking—federal holiday notwithstanding—is a lone camper at the Round Bottom horse camp along Straight Fork Road.

Rather than set out on Hyatt Ridge Trail, I start hiking about 1⅓ miles up Straight Fork Road to Beech Gap Trail (western section). By doing so, I'll be able to loop back to the car via Hyatt Ridge and Beech Gap Trails. Before completing the loop, I also plan to travel out and back about two miles on Enloe Creek Trail, so that I can hike down to Raven Fork and then up to a crossing of Enloe Creek. Although the route comprises about 11½ miles, I'll be exploring only a relatively small part of the vast and isolated Raven Fork watershed.

After covering the stretch of Straight Fork Road on foot in less than a half hour—enjoying morning sunlight and splashes of fall color along the way—I turn left on Beech Gap Trail, just before a stout bridge crosses Straight Fork. (The trailhead for the eastern section of Beech Gap Trail, the section that in fact leads to Beech Gap, is located beyond the bridge.) Right away, the trail climbs above Straight Fork on a moderate grade with the path cushioned by fallen leaves. In just a few minutes, nearly total silence prevails, the sounds of the stream left behind as the trail climbs away from it. After just over two miles, the path reaches a level, open area or slight gap; trail guides use the term "false gap" to describe the spot. False or not, it harbors a huge oak tree and a nice log that begs me to take a short rest. The final push to the junction with Hyatt Ridge Trail is generally easygoing, as most of the ascent is completed at this point.

Soon, I arrive at the junction with Hyatt Ridge Trail. At nearly five thousand feet in elevation, this is the highest altitude I'll attain today. It's a lovely spot for an early lunch, with beautiful red spruce mixed among large and small hardwoods. A slight breeze chills the late-morning air as I see a bit of fiery fall color through the forest. There's even an ideal place to sit: an upright section of a large fallen tree that was sawed after it blocked the trail. I'm tempted to follow Hyatt Ridge Trail past 5,137-foot Hyatt Bald to the path's terminus at McGee Spring backcountry campsite, but I'm on a mission to reach Raven Fork, so I decide to head in that direction on the trail.

As I hike on Hyatt Ridge Trail toward Raven Fork, I'm treated to more peeks at fall color, visible along the upper reaches of Balsam Mountain to my left and Hyatt Ridge to my rear right. At one slight break in the trees, I see what I think is the more distant Plott Balsam Range. The descending trail becomes steeper, rockier, and eroded in places as I near the junction with Enloe Creek Trail, the path that will take me down to the highly anticipated Raven Fork. There's no hint at the expansive trail junction that less than a mile away is a hard-charging stream that's almost deafening when its churning water is high.

The descent to Raven Fork from the junction of Enloe Creek and Hyatt Ridge Trails is moderately steep, dropping from about forty-four hundred to under thirty-eight hundred feet in roughly a mile. In less than a half-mile, I hear the first distant sounds of the roaring fork. Farther down, I cross a Raven Fork tributary, just beyond a short trail section shored by a wooden support rather than riprap. Soon after the fork comes into view, the trail makes its final approach to the stream via three tight switchbacks. The path arrives streamside just downstream from a steel bridge, whose span is about fifteen feet higher than the water level on this dry October day.

Even with low water, Raven Fork is thrilling in its untamed wildness. Rushing water churns and cascades into beautiful clear pools, situated amid boulders that, in some cases, are bigger than the biggest trucks and SUVs Detroit can build. I carefully step out onto one boulder, and then another, in order to get better views looking upstream; Breakneck Ridge soars a few miles to the north. Later, as I cross the bridge, I notice that a few hemlock trees have established a home atop one of the massive boulders. Even with the man-made structure, the wilderness scene here is extraordinary.

On the far side of the bridge, I arrive at a cozy backcountry campsite, curiously named Enloe Creek rather than Raven Fork, even though Enloe Creek flows into Raven Fork some distance downstream. Perhaps the Enloes had a better PR person than the ravens, Edgar Allan Poe notwithstanding. It's a scenic, if small, campsite where one would hope to have considerate neighbors at such close range. Then again, with high water, the roar of Raven Fork probably drowns out all but the noisiest of campers.

Speaking of high water, the Enloe Creek campsite is not a place where one would wish to camp if there were the slightest chance of intense rainfall in a short period of time, as the steep watershed occasionally creates a wall of water rushing through the gorge. The site has the usual food-cable system, but it's attached to the bridge rather than suspended between trees. A loftier storage option is available nearby, courtesy of a tall pole with hooks at the top, but anyone shorter than six feet tall would likely have trouble hoisting a pack onto any of them.

After resting on a log next to one of the permanent fire rings, I continue on Enloe Creek Trail, which initially climbs sharply above the campsite. I begin to hear, but don't see, Enloe Creek to my left as it tumbles toward its meeting with Raven Fork. Soon after the creek becomes visible through the vegetation, I spot several lovely small falls and cascades. The trail crosses the creek about a mile above Raven Fork, but because the footbridge has washed out, I decide not to attempt a tricky (and wet) rock-hop across the stream—it's no longer summertime, and I have nearly four miles of hiking back to the car as it is. On my way back down to Raven Fork, I hear a commotion in the woods above me, but I'm unable to see what kind of animal is causing it. In a few minutes, I enjoy one last look at the fork as I cross it on the bridge and begin the stiff climb out of the gorge.

The last leg of today's excursion is the final piece of Hyatt Ridge Trail, a mostly steep and rocky course that takes me down to my car on Straight Fork Road. I cross and then hike above Hyatt Creek as it too makes its way to Straight Fork. The Hyatt finale concludes a day of solitude, as well as quietude, except for the sounds of streams and occasional breezes. The remote Raven Fork section of the park truly is "wild lonesome up thar," but no, not too much so on a golden autumn day.

Hike 33

Chasing Fall Color

October 17
Trails: Balsam Mountain,
    Mount Sterling Ridge
Trailhead weather
    conditions: 61 degrees,
    partly cloudy, calm
Round-trip miles hiked: 14.6

The towering Balsam Mountain Range stretches from south of the park to the Great Smokies' crest at Tricorner Knob. Although the Blue Ridge Parkway follows the muscular Balsams outside the park, the trailhead for Balsam Mountain Trail is one of the remotest in the Smokies. A one-way gravel road, departing from Heintooga Picnic Area, leads to the trailhead at Pin Oak Gap, Balsam Mountain's lowest point inside the park at an elevation just above forty-four hundred feet. From the gap, the trail runs for about ten miles before reaching its Tricorner Knob terminus at approximately six thousand feet in elevation. Today I plan to hike to the vicinity of another corner—Balsam Corner—where I intend to take a right onto the western end of Mount Sterling Ridge Trail and follow that path for a few miles. This excursion coincides with what will likely be close to the height of fall color in the park's upper elevations.

If all goes as planned, today's outing will bring me to more than three hundred fifty miles of hiking in the Smokies for the year. It may be my last hike of 2016 that exceeds five thousand feet in elevation, because as cooler weather approaches, I'll begin to aim for lower-elevation routes. This year's crazily dry and warm weather overall has certainly worked to my advantage while I've explored the spectacular Smokies' high country.

Along the drive out Heintooga Ridge Road toward the park boundary at Black Camp Gap, I come upon a convention of elk in and along the road—or more specifically, about a dozen cows, though I don't spot a bull for the apparent harem. I stop to allow the crowd to clear the road safely. On the other side of the gap, an almost equal number of wild turkeys scatter along the road. But I see the morning's most surprising sight several miles later, after I've parked to walk out to Heintooga Overlook: three young women camping at the picnic area. I learn that the trio, on fall break from a college in Tennessee, had apparently planned to spend the night at nearby Balsam Mountain Campground, only to find it closed for the season. But they assure me they have a backcountry camping permit for tonight at the Caldwell Fork site in Cataloochee Valley. When they ask where they can find water—the picnic ground's restrooms and spigots are also shut down—I tell them that Flat Creek about a mile away is likely the best bet unless they can find someone at the ranger residence near the campground entrance. But they cheerfully say they have enough water to make it to Caldwell Fork. I hope they're right, because they'll be traveling about 8½ miles on foot on a warm October day.

After walking out to enjoy the slightly murky morning views from Heintooga Overlook, I return to the car and start the serpentine drive to the Balsam Mountain trailhead at Pin Oak Gap. A sign for the one-way road notes that it's twenty-eight miles to Cherokee, but the route makes it seem several times that because more than half that distance is on a narrow gravel surface. From here, I'll have about 8½ miles and a half-hour of driving to the trailhead, but fine views and fall color compensate for the somewhat grueling drive.

Is it really mid-October? Upon my arrival at the trailhead, my thermometer reads sixty-one degrees here at more than forty-four hundred feet in elevation. Surely that temperature at 9:15 A.M. already exceeds the average high reading at this altitude for October 17. Still, it's hard to complain about another balmy day for a long hike in the Smokies. But even if I were hiking in a cold, driving rain, I doubt I would grumble about my latest backcountry escape from the coarseness of an R-rated, celebrity-driven presidential campaign that mercifully will end in about three weeks—I think.

Just past a former gate, I begin ascending on the trail, which soon levels on a good tread, mostly free of rocks and roots. It's pleasant hiking while I enjoy the fine weather and some nice autumn color—mostly yellows and golds at this elevation. In an area with stands of stately red spruce, I see evidence of extensive rooting by wild boar on either side of the trail. Several wild turkeys scatter while I make my way up the trail. The path does a dance with Swain and Haywood Counties, as Balsam Mountain separates the two inside the park before running into Tennessee around Tricorner Knob. After 1½ miles or so, the trail gets serious about climbing as it begins a rather stiff ascent to 5,184-foot Ledge Bald, which is now forested like nearly all the peaks in the Smokies named balds. From here, I start hiking the short distance down to Beech Gap, which lies about one hundred feet lower than Ledge Bald.

Beech Gap, once known as Big Swag, was an expansive grazing area for livestock into the 1930s. Now populated by beech and other northern hardwoods, as well as a scattering of red spruce, the broad area has the feel of a leafy urban park. Old rail grades, vestiges of the timber companies, are located on either side of the gap. These days, Beech Gap provides an excellent way station of sorts, complete with resting logs, before Balsam Mountain Trail begins a stiff climb that skirts the summit of Balsam High Top, which tops out at about fifty-seven hundred feet.

As I continue on the trail at around fifty-five hundred feet in elevation, I start to notice some Fraser firs mixing with red spruce. Clouds, one of Balsam Mountain's calling cards, begin to build, but today they're not going to produce any rain. I walk across a series of planks, which are laid on the trail through here to provide boardwalks over typically muddy areas chewed up by horses. Today the planked areas are dry, until I reach a quagmire near Laurel Gap backcountry shelter, after a sharp descent from the shoulder of Balsam High Top.

Laurel Gap shelter is situated in an attractive glade, where there's a horse hitching post in addition to the usual food cables and metal fire ring; water is available nearby. Built by the Youth Conservation Corps in the late 1960s, the shelter was renovated several years ago and remains in good, clean condition. In this quiet setting, with predictably no one around at midday, I eat one of the two sandwiches I've packed, before rejoining Balsam Mountain Trail for a short distance.

At a junction a few minutes up the trail, I turn right onto Mount Sterling Ridge Trail. From here for about three miles, the Sterling path is about as flat as a trail in the floodplain of Congaree National Park south of Columbia, South Carolina, despite being roughly fifty-five hundred feet higher in elevation than any trail in Congaree. Rather than following the ridgeline, which includes 6,155-foot Big Cataloochee Mountain, Mount Sterling Ridge Trail runs on a remarkably level course, below the crest on this three-mile stretch. The trail traverses the headwaters of Lost Bottom and Cooks Creeks, as well as pockets of evergreen among the high-elevation northern hardwoods. Some adventurous hikers might dismiss the section as too easy or even boring. But I find it anything but dull; perhaps I'm easily amused. As the trail finally starts to descend toward Pretty Hollow Gap, I realize that I'm about as far from a road—paved or unpaved—as I've been all year. It would take about three hours on foot to reach any road. Especially without reliable cell service, blowing out a knee or ankle this far back in the woods would not produce a good chain of events.

I turn back toward Balsam Mountain Trail. I reach it in about an hour, soon after taking in one particularly distant view at a break in the trees to my left. The trail sign at the junction notes the distance to Laural [sic] Gap shelter as three-tenths mile, but it's actually only about three hundred yards. When I arrive back at the shelter, I notice that a thermometer on one of its rock walls has a reading of seventy-five degrees. The one time I camped here, in early October 1985, overnight temperatures dipped below freezing. After hiking back up to the slopes of Balsam High Top, I enjoy the descent to Beech Gap, where mid-afternoon sunlight is pouring through the forest. Typical Balsam Mountain breezes freshen during the slightly more than two miles from here back to the car. These breezes are nothing like the fierce winds that will whip across the mountain when the first real cold front of the season blows in from the Dakotas or someplace. Once again, I've not seen any other hikers on the trail today.

Driving down toward Cherokee on the remaining five miles or so of the one-way gravel road, I'm stunned to see something I've previously not seen on Balsam Mountain Road: someone driving in the opposite direction. And in a massive SUV, no less. I lean outside my window to tell the driver he's driving the wrong way on a one-way road, and that there's another vehicle not far behind me. I maneuver around the SUV and assume the driver soon got turned around without incident. Wrong-way driving, illegal camping—ah, just another October day in Great Smoky Mountains National Park.

Hike 34

Toward Balsam Mountain—from Cataloochee

October 19
Trails: Pretty Hollow Gap, Palmer Creek
Trailhead weather conditions: 72 degrees, partly cloudy, calm
Round-trip miles hiked: 9.8

The isolated Cataloochee Valley, though only about ten miles from a heavily traveled interstate highway, was a lightly visited part of the park until the reintroduction of the American elk into the valley. Now well established in the valley and a few other places in the Smokies, the imposing animals draw throngs of people into Cataloochee despite a difficult drive on serpentine roads. Today Karen and I intrepidly join the valley's October crowds, as we plan to hike what may be my favorite path in Cataloochee: Palmer Creek Trail. From its trailhead about 1½ miles along Pretty Hollow Gap Trail, Palmer Creek Trail works its way up to Balsam Mountain Road in about 3⅓ miles on a pleasant course, favored by lovely streams and a mix of forest types, which today exhibit showy fall color.

Like most trails in Cataloochee Valley, Palmer Creek Trail is open to horse traffic, even though the path is tight much of the way. But I don't recall seeing much traffic of any kind—equine or human—on previous hikes on the trail that mostly stays well above Palmer Creek itself. It traverses a narrow valley pinched by Butt Mountain and Beech Ridge to the north and by the abruptly rising Shanty Mountain to the south. Although the path climbs about fifteen hundred feet from trailhead to terminus, at no point does its grade become more than moderately steep. The ascent is gradual on a generally good tread.

Forget Indian summer—today feels more like plain old summer, even though the elk's early-autumn rut, accompanied by high-pitched bugling, has come and gone. The high in Asheville today will reach eighty-four degrees, a record for the date. Here in "Catalooch," temps in and around the valley floor will also touch the eighties, with plenty of sun. The tortuous drive up and over Cove Creek Gap into the valley is about as dusty as I've ever seen it, as the Smokies continue to be parched. The fall fire season officially began a few days ago, and it's shaping up to be a serious one. But I have no complaints about today's weather for hiking.

We begin walking on Pretty Hollow Gap Trail, which is initially a gravel road, leading to a horse camp in about one-fourth mile. Picturesque Palmer Creek is to our left, even though we won't reach Palmer Creek Trail for more than a half hour. Pretty Hollow Gap Trail narrows once we clear the well-populated horse camp to the right of the road. In a few places, the path is rocky and briefly steep, but it's mostly easy hiking until the junction with Palmer Creek Trail about three-fourths mile past the start of Little Cataloochee Trail.

After seeing a lone hiker at the junction, just above the confluence of Palmer and Pretty Hollow Creeks, we cross the latter on a foot log, which heralds the start of Palmer Creek Trail. The wide, flat area adjoining the creek is known as Indian Flats, long ago the site of a Cherokee camp. But it doesn't take long for the trail to commence climbing, as it has quite a bit of work to do in order to reach an elevation of forty-five hundred feet at Balsam Mountain Road. En route, the trail travels through cove hardwood, closed oak, and northern hardwood forests, each displaying beautiful fall color. As we start ascending, leaves flutter toward the forest floor, ready to begin the process of decomposing. One hazard, at least on horse trails, of fallen leaves and the softer footing they provide is that horse manure is harder to spot. But fortunately, we will see little of that today.

Slightly more than a mile up the trail, we reach a crossing of Lost Bottom Creek, a Palmer Creek tributary whose headwaters I encountered just a couple of days ago on Mount Sterling Ridge Trail about two thousand feet higher in elevation. Fortunately, there's a foot log, as even with low water a rock-hop crossing looks a bit risky. But we're on our own about one half-mile farther up the trail where Palmer Creek Trail crosses Beech Creek—the foot log noted in trail guides was apparently swept away at some point. We rely on a couple of large boulders to make it across the creek, which merges with Falling Rock Creek a short distance downstream to form Palmer Creek. From here, the trail roughly parallels Falling Rock Creek, which courses well below the path, for the remaining 1¾ miles or so to Balsam Mountain Road. A few minutes above Beech Creek, we stop for lunch, after spotting a couple of comfortable logs to sit on to the left of the path.

Near the terminus, soon after as lead hiker, I see a ruffed grouse take flight straight up the trail. Rhododendron encloses the path for about one hundred yards before the trail levels off as it slips onto an old rail grade. To the left (south) are some nice views of Spruce Mountain, a prominent peak rising to an elevation of 5,647 feet near the merger of Shanty Mountain and Spruce Mountain Ridge. There is a small backcountry campsite near the summit of Spruce Mountain, which is reached via a short trail farther up Balsam Mountain Road. A fire tower that once stood atop this summit was removed long ago.

Above and to the right of the trail's end is equipment that, at times, could save lives in the Raven Fork and Cataloochee Creek watersheds, far below its lofty location. It's a rainfall-monitoring site, which serves as a flood-warning station for the Straight Fork and Raven Fork areas to the southwest and for the Cataloochee Creek drainage to the east—all of which are prone to flash flooding with their steep watersheds in high-rainfall areas. Early warning is especially critical in regard to Straight and Raven Forks, as those streams converge and flow through the populated Big Cove area of the Cherokee Indian Reservation. The flood-warning equipment includes a precipitation gauge, solar panel, and radio antenna mounted on a standpipe within a fenced enclosure. The station was established through collaboration among the North Carolina Department of Public Safety, National Weather Service, and National Park Service.

I decide to walk out on my own to the trail's end at Balsam Mountain Road, the terminus I drove past earlier this week on my way to Pin Oak Gap and Balsam Mountain Trail. I eat a quick snack while resting on one of the boulders, which are more than large enough to prevent anyone from driving a vehicle onto the old rail grade. An SUV on Balsam Mountain Road rumbles past, headed in the right direction, unlike the one I saw farther down the road two days ago. The vehicle has about ten more miles of slow, but scenic, travel on a winding gravel road. With luck, the driver won't meet anyone driving the wrong way.

Soon it's time to head back to the valley floor. As we hike down Palmer Creek Trail, we enjoy stunning fall color on parts of Shanty Mountain, spoiled only by countless dead hemlock trees among the mountain's colorful hardwoods. As we approach Palmer Creek, we see two late-afternoon hikers headed up the trail. They will need to set a good pace if they're planning to make it all the way to Balsam Mountain Road and back by nightfall.

We're back at the car by 4:30 P.M., ready to drive back to Interstate 40. We meet quite a few vehicles while we drive out on the twisting road, as visitors stream into the valley for late-day elk viewing, but fortunately encounter only a couple of large RVs. The calendar says October, but it's been a nice summer-like day in one of the park's loveliest areas.

Hike 35

Skirting Mount Cammerer

October 28
Trail: Lower Mount Cammerer
Trailhead weather conditions: 67 degrees, sunny, calm
Round-trip miles hiked: 15.0

With four October hikes already in the books, I had planned to round out my year of hiking with three outings in November and three more in December. But with the weather so good (or bad, considering the worsening drought), daylight saving time still in effect, and fall color lingering, I can't resist another excursion or two this month. So I decide to set out for Cosby Campground in the northeastern corner of the park for my second short front-country camping trip of the year, just ahead of the campground's November 1 closing. Two nights out will give me an opportunity to hike at least two more trails in Tennessee, pushing me past sixty in the Smokies for the year. That will leave me with just four more hikes to accomplish in 2016, instead of hiking six during the limited-daylight days of November and December. I'm like the forest animals that gather food for the winter, except that I'm collecting hikes.

Today's adventure takes me on the lengthy Lower Mount Cammerer Trail. Unlike the short, but rugged, Mount Cammerer Trail that follows the mountain's spine at about five thousand feet, Lower Mount Cammerer Trail swings around Cammerer's lower-elevation contours, coursing well below its summit. The lower cousin's distance also is about twelve times longer: 7.4 miles vs. 0.6 mile. Although the longer trail lacks the dramatic views of the shorter path, it does feature a short spur trail that leads to an impressive lookout. Lower Mount Cammerer Trail also offers a pleasant woodland walk on a path that's easy on the feet. In fact, unlike many paths in the Smokies, the trail is mostly free of rocks, roots, and—at least during a drought—muddy sections.

After making camp midmorning at an attractive site near the trailhead for Snake Den Ridge Trail (see Hike 15), I walk across Cosby Campground's upper loop to reach the Lower Mount Cammerer trailhead, just past an access to Low Gap Trail. My chosen path soon crosses Cosby Creek on a foot log and continues to follow an old roadbed past a junction with the seemingly ubiquitous Low Gap Trail. The woods are almost eerily still and quiet for a while, until the silence is broken by a pileated woodpecker and then by a jet. The trail narrows before crossing Toms Creek on a foot log. After clearing the branch, the trail follows a dry ridge, which gently ascends to a short side trail leading to Sutton Ridge Overlook. (Perhaps "lookout" is a more accurate term.) There's a hitching rack here because the steep, rocky spur to the lookout isn't suitable for horse traffic. I climb the two hundred yards or so to the view spot, where I meet two local residents at the small clearing. Not wishing to intrude, I decide to depart after a couple of minutes, with the expectation of climbing back up here on my way back to camp later in the day.

Upon my return to the main path, I resume hiking on a mostly gentle grade, which takes me in and out of several draws and coves over the next six miles or so. This gentle grade has a net elevation gain of barely one thousand feet. From the Sutton Ridge spur, though, the trail drops rather sharply before climbing a dry ridge, affording nice views to the west. In a couple of more miles, I reach Gilliland Creek backcountry camp, which actually consists of a lower site for those on foot and an upper site for those on horseback. For a lunch spot I choose the lower area, wedged between a ridge and the currently thirsty Gilliland Fork (not Creek).

In proceeding after lunch toward a junction with the Appalachian Trail, I traverse a series of ridges: Leadmine, Rowdy, and Groundhog. After the only significant ascent, I'm surprised to be greeted by another solo hiker, who as it turns out also lives in Asheville. He says he's planning to hike a long loop that will take him up the Appalachian Trail to the Mount Cammerer spur trail and fire tower before he heads back to Cosby via the AT and Low Gap Trail. As I walk ahead of him, I tell him I'm tempted to do the same, despite the additional climbing and distance, even though I hiked to the tower earlier in the month. The Cammerer lookout truly is a jaw-dropping spot anytime the elements are favorable, as they certainly are today.

After another half hour or so of easy and enjoyable hiking, I reach a familiar intersection with the Appalachian Trail, about one mile above the AT's junction with the Chestnut Branch Trail, which I hiked a few weeks ago. I've been through here several times previously, but never after hiking up from Cosby on Lower Cammerer Trail. It's a good place for a rest stop, though it can be busy during the spring AT "thru-hiker" season. On my somewhat lengthy stay, the only people who pass through today are a couple of day hikers, on their way down from Mount Cammerer fire tower, and the Asheville solo hiker, who turns right (south) toward the Cammerer spur trail.

Around three o'clock, it's time to pack up and head back toward Cosby, as I have nearly three hours of hiking ahead of me, as well as supper to prepare before the late-October darkness envelops the campground. On my way down, at the same spot where I initially spoke with the solo hiker, I see a couple of backpackers who seem to be setting up shop in a level, open area about seventy-five feet to the right of the trail. Perhaps they are simply resting for a while and not planning to establish a rogue backcountry campsite for the night. Later, as I near the Gilliland Creek camp, two more backpackers, whom I'd seen on my way to the AT, are heading back in that direction, noting that they're looking for water. Actually there's a bit of water at the backcountry campsite, where I later notice a couple of backpacks that have been dropped. Nearby, I also spot a mound of bear scat on the trail, perhaps an ominous sign since the abandoned packs would likely be of great interest to a bear.

The highlight on the hike back to my Cosby Campground home for the next two nights will be the return to Sutton Ridge lookout, which I hope I'll have to myself for a few minutes. As I start climbing out of a cove toward the spur trail, a friendly young hiker approaches and asks, "Are you going to the lookout? I took some pictures." I assure him that, yes, I plan to make the short side trip up there. This time, no one is at the lookout and won't be for the ten or fifteen minutes I linger. The view looking west toward the Smokies' crest and 5,940-foot-high Inadu Knob is especially dramatic, though to enjoy it I have to squint into a blinding afternoon sun—Stephen Crane's "fierce wafer" in a vastly different context. It's an unexpectedly thrilling vista, considering the heavily forested character of Lower Mount Cammerer Trail.

Hiking back on the final 1½ miles or so of the main trail, I'm not surprised to see several hikers out for what are likely afternoon strolls before supper. It's easy walking the rest of the way, punctuated by the two foot logs and the Low Gap Trail junction. Even with the side trip to Sutton Ridge Overlook, I make it back to camp before six o'clock, giving me just enough daylight to fix a hot meal of potatoes, baked beans, and grilled burgers—certainly nothing elaborate, but filling and satisfying after a long day on the trail. I'll settle in for the night in my tent by about 8:30, hoping to sleep well before a shorter, but more strenuous, hike tomorrow in the nearby Greenbrier section of the park. And for better or for worse considering the fire danger, I needn't worry about overnight rain pelting my tent and fly—there's no chance of precipitation anytime soon, according to the weather forecast. The drought persists across the Smokies.

Hike 36

On Top of Old . . . Brushy

October 29
Trails: Porters Creek, Brushy
   Mountain
*Trailhead weather
   conditions:* 57 degrees,
   fair, calm
Round-trip miles hiked: 11.8

The spring wildflower display along Porters Creek Trail is considered one of the finest in the Smokies. After missing out on that showy season earlier in the year, I finally make it to Porters Creek today. It's my second trip of the year to the Greenbrier section of the park; the previous one was exactly eight months earlier on the February 29 quadrennial for a late-winter hike to Ramsey Cascades. My timing for that excursion was much better, as Ramsey Cascades Trail closed about five months later, when a large tree fell and damaged a vital foot log crossing Ramsey Prong, rendering the creek crossing impassable. (The extremely popular trail remained closed several months into 2017.) And vehicle access to the Greenbrier section itself will be halted for a while in November for much-needed repairs to road bridges. But on this brilliant October day, Porters Creek Trail is clear for takeoff. The same goes for Brushy Mountain Trail, which I plan to veer off on after about one mile when I reach an area known as Porters Flat. The Brushy Mountain Trail climbs steadily for nearly five miles until it reaches the summit of Brushy Mountain, rising to an elevation above forty-nine hundred feet on the northern spur of brawny Mount Le Conte. It's a formidable hike, gaining well over twenty-five hundred feet in elevation on its lengthy ascent from Porters Creek. The contrast in ecosystems is notable as well.

I'm off the mark early—just after daybreak—from my Cosby campsite for the drive of slightly more than a half hour to the Porters Creek trailhead. Only three cars are parked at the spacious parking area when I arrive about eight o'clock. But within about five minutes of my arrival, two other vehicles pull in, one carrying hikers and the other a fisherman. It's pleasantly cool as I embark on Porters Creek Trail; a warming sun won't pop into view over nearby Bald Top Ridge until after I connect with Brushy Mountain Trail. With the creek to my left, I hike on an old roadbed through a rather spindly second-growth forest. Less than a mile from the start, on the right after a foot log over Long Branch, stone steps lead up to a small cemetery well above the creek. I soon reach a wide road turnaround and the junction with Brushy Mountain Trail, where there's a shady grove of hemlock trees. Trail signs direct me to the right, and then almost immediately to the left for Brushy Mountain Trail. On the other side of the turnaround, a historic barn and cabin are easily reached, but because I'm on a mission to start climbing out of the Porters Creek Valley toward my lofty destination, I decide to bypass those structures until my return from Brushy Mountain.

As Brushy Mountain Trail departs the Porters Flat area, it passes a stone wall from an old homesite on the left and runs near the oddly named Fittified Spring, so labeled because the spring supposedly began flowing "in fits" in the early twentieth century. Farther up the trail, there's a tangle of large fallen hardwoods on the right, perhaps victims of a fierce storm. The path continues on a moderate grade through an open forest for several more minutes, until I reach a switchback that heralds a short section of trail that passes several large poplars. I see bright fall foliage on Grapeyard Ridge to the north-

west. Soon the trail swings back to the right onto a dry, sun-baked ridge, where pines predictably mix with the hardwoods. From the ridge, I enjoy fine views of part of the soaring Smokies' crest and of Greenbrier Pinnacle, an east-west ridge abruptly rising to an elevation of about forty-eight hundred feet. A fire tower once stood on its western end.

The trail climbs steadily on a generally straight course until its character changes when it traverses a damp, dark cove where Trillium Branch flows. As I veer left to rock-hop across the branch, Trillium Gap, at roughly forty-seven hundred feet in elevation, isn't far above me to the west. To get there, the trail turns southeast for a while before another switchback redirects the path back toward the gap. I see several hemlock skeletons through here, but after the trail doubles back toward Trillium Gap, I'm treated to a few peeks at brilliant fall color along the southern flank of Brushy Mountain—color that strikes me as unusually vivid for late October at such a high elevation. The gap seems elusive as I continue along the rocky, leaf-covered trail, but once red spruce start to appear on either side of the path I know Trillium Gap can't be too far away. I hear voices below me, apparently from other hikers who are making their way up from Porters Creek, though I won't see them until a few minutes after I reach the summit.

Finally, I reach the gap, a busy place at times because Trillium Gap Trail, a popular path that originates near Gatlinburg, also runs through here on its way to Mount Le Conte. Even though I got an early start and made good time from Greenbrier, I'm surprised to find no one at the gap upon my arrival. A trail sign notes that it's just two-tenths mile to Brushy Mountain, but I discover that the final leg to the top is more like twice that distance as the path ascends another two hundred feet or so in elevation.

In addition to being steep in places, the trail to

the summit of Brushy Mountain is basically a rocky trough in places, punctuated in spots by horse manure. Although trail maps indicate that this last stretch of Brushy Mountain Trail is open to hikers only, there's no question that horses have been through here in recent days. But soon, the trail emerges from its badly eroded sections and leaves the forest behind as well, arriving on the lofty heath bald, where vegetation such as laurel, rhododendron, sand myrtle, and crunchy lichens predominate—vestiges of at least one fire that swept across the mountain before the park was established. The absence of trees, except for one lonely pine and a colorful large hardwood farther off the trail, allows for some remarkable views atop the mountain.

I continue along what is now an easy path to the northern part of Brushy, before doubling back to an annex of sorts just off the trail, which seems to be the best perch near the summit. Although a couple of rocks have been placed in order to provide a well-positioned seat, I decide to stack two nearby larger ones (there's also a brick in the area, oddly enough) in order to create a slightly higher vantage point while enjoying a bite of lunch. I can see numerous prominent peaks from here, including Myrtle Point, High Top, and Cliff Top on Mount Le Conte; Mount Kephart, Charlies Bunion, The Sawteeth, Mount Guyot, and Cosby Knob along the Smokies' crest; and Greenbrier Pinnacle, rising just beyond the Middle Prong of the Little Pigeon River. Dramatically below this point is the Porters Creek watershed, where I began today's excursion about three hours ago. With the exception of Mount Le Conte, the views from Brushy Mountain likely rival those of any summit in the park not located along the Smokies' crest.

After a few minutes, a young couple apparently determines that I indeed have the best vantage point on the mountain and decide to join me at the small clearing. In turn, I tell them that I'm leaving the view spot to them, as I've been here for a while already. The gesture seems more expected than appreciated, but that's fine as I find another opening along the trail toward Trillium Gap, where I can briefly set up shop, soaking up the October sun. It's another blue-sky afternoon, broken only by a few high clouds, with excellent long-range visibility, in addition to closer views of impressive fall color this late in the month. A couple of gregarious hikers, likely the ones I heard below Trillium Gap, pass by my spot and comment on what a terrific, if little touted, peak Brushy Mountain is, especially considering its proximity to frenzied Gatlinburg. In fact, Brushy is not even identified on the venerable Knoxville relief map, even though it exceeds the elevations of some of the other mountains, such as Greenbrier Pinnacle, that are on that map.

I soon start hiking back toward Trillium Gap, fortunate to clear the trench-like sections before meeting a group of hikers headed toward the summit. I again have the gap to myself for a couple of minutes before I continue on Brushy Mountain Trail. Because fallen leaves obscure rocks and exposed roots, the descent is somewhat tricky until I complete the two switchbacks and cross Trillium Branch. I make better time on the dry ridge after the branch, and soon approach the Porters Flat area. This time, I make the short side trip to the cantilevered John Messer Barn, circa 1875, and the old Smoky Mountains Hiking Club Cabin, built in the mid-1930s and used by the club for nearly a half-century through an agreement with the park service. Between the two structures is a sizable springhouse.

I see a steady stream of hikers and backpackers on the walk of less than a half hour from Porters Flat back to the trailhead parking area. In contrast to early this morning, the large parking area is now spilling over with vehicles on this warm Saturday afternoon. Not surprisingly, the traffic is heavy as I drive out of

Greenbrier on narrow, bumpy roads. These visitors and I are among the more than ten million people (unofficial count) who visited the Smokies during the first ten months of 2016. Although the hike to Old Brushy—OK, so the folk song's title is actually "On Top of Old Smoky," not Brushy—was undeniably rewarding, I'm looking forward to returning to the quieter Cosby area and a restful weekend camp amid considerate neighbors.

Hike 37

Trails to Somewhere

November 10
Trails: Lakeshore, Whiteoak Branch, Forney Creek, Bear Creek, Tunnel Bypass
Trailhead weather conditions: 48 degrees, sunny, calm
Round-trip miles hiked: 9.6

After easily the most dismal—not to mention disturbing—presidential campaign of my baby-boomer lifetime, I admit to post-election shell shock. Perhaps there's no better way to deal with it short-term than with an autumn outing in the park. But my eagerness to answer the call of the woods today is somewhat blunted by the reality the mountains are in a severe-to-extreme drought that has led to numerous wildfires and pockets of dense smoke, even if forestland in the Smokies has been spared to date. A ban on campfires in the Smokies' backcountry, which began ten days ago, may have helped prevent forest fires in the park thus far. (*Footnote*: By mid-November, with tinder-dry conditions even worse, park officials institute a ban on all fires in the park that continues for more than a month.) The Smokies badly need a steady, soaking rain, but the weather forecast offers little hope the persistent dryness will end anytime soon. So once again, I'm starting a hike in mostly fair weather, as I have nearly all year.

Anyone who enters the park via Lake View Drive outside Bryson City comes upon a strange sight when the road plays out after several miles: a long tunnel beyond the point where vehicle access ends. The road and tunnel—all twelve hundred linear feet of it—are the legacy of road construction along the North Shore of Fontana Lake that was halted nearly a half-century ago because of mounting environmental and economic concerns. As a result, many local residents, especially those whose families were displaced by the creation of Fontana Lake in the early 1940s, refer to Lake View Drive as The Road to Nowhere. Even Bryson City street signs note it as such. The raw feelings stem from a 1943 agreement in which the federal government agreed to build a new road along Fontana Lake's North Shore to replace state highway 288, which was substantially submerged by the lake when Fontana Dam was completed in late 1944. The lingering bitterness among many local residents, particularly those who have relatives buried in North Shore cemeteries, is on full display on a sign that greets motorists just outside the park boundary:

WELCOME TO
THE ROAD TO NO-WHERE
A BROKEN PROMISE!
1943-?
NO MORE WILDERNESS

But if it doesn't go to its initially planned destination near Fontana Dam, Lake View Drive does indeed go somewhere within the park, just as numerous relatively short roads in the Smokies do. Thus, The Tunnel to Nowhere might be a more apt label since major construction did create a tunnel that ultimately did go nowhere. There's even a horse and hiking path called Tunnel Bypass Trail, for those who don't wish to ride horseback or walk (and maybe step in something) through the long, dark tunnel in order to work their way west toward Forney Creek. In fact, I plan to take the bypass trail myself on my return to the car this afternoon.

Enduring road controversy notwithstanding, travel along the winding Lake View Drive on this sunny fall morning is beautiful and peaceful. I'm surprised to encounter no other vehicles on the five-mile drive from the park boundary to the large parking area, located just before a poled barricade near the tunnel entrance. Even this deep into November, I see splashes of fall color as sunlight pours into the forest. I also notice, on my first visit here since the late 1990s, that parts of the road construction required considerable rock blasting, as the unfinished road sections surely would have as well. I travel across a long, curving bridge span crossing Noland Creek and drive the short distance to the parking lot, where my car joins a truck and horse trailer as the only vehicles.

Upon exiting the car, I'm approached by a young backpacker, who has just emerged from the dark walk through the tunnel. I'm thinking he may be planning to ask me for a ride to somewhere, just as I did with an obliging motorist here about thirty years ago. But no, he has a much weightier question after being away from civilization for a while:

"Excuse me. Could you tell me who won the election?" he asks earnestly.

He looks stunned—almost ashen—when I tell him. I learn he's been mostly out of touch since starting the three-hundred-mile Benton MacKaye Trail at Springer Mountain, Georgia, where the storied Appalachian Trail also begins. The adventurer is on his way to Noland Creek Trail, just down the road from here, as he continues a journey that will end in a few days at Big Creek in the northeastern part of the park. We chat for a few minutes, and I wish him the best on the remainder of his travels—and on the next four years.

By the time we've finished talking, another car has

arrived at the parking area. A man and woman get out and start walking through the tunnel, which has no shortage of graffiti despite its darkness. I catch up with them just beyond the far end of the tunnel, near where the road pavement ends for good, and quickly receive another pertinent question:

"Do you know why they would build a tunnel and then end the road just past it?" the man asks. Obviously the correct answer isn't so that tunnel art could be created.

"How much time do you have?" I reply, only half-jokingly. I then share the CliffsNotes version of the long-running road saga, which still isn't resolved, even though the federal government agreed in 2007 to pay Swain County $52 million in lieu of the road. A decade later, the government has paid only $12.8 million. The couple seems just slightly less incredulous than the backpacker was upon hearing the election news. We wish each other well as we all continue much shorter journeys than that of the MacKaye hiker.

Initially, I'm hiking on part of the thirty-five-mile Lakeshore Trail, which does in fact stretch from the infamous tunnel to within a mile of Fontana Dam. It's one of several trails I plan to travel today, as I aim to complete a figure-eight route of nearly ten miles that will bring me to a total of four hundred trail miles in the Smokies for the year. Although the winter solstice is now just six weeks away, I should still have plenty of daylight to finish my planned hike because I set out about 10:45 A.M.

At the outset, Lakeshore Trail is not only dry, but also dusty in places where there's no leaf cover. It soon crosses the lower end of Forney Ridge, trading the Noland Creek watershed for that of Forney Creek. Through the trees are some nice views of Welch Ridge, crowned by the nearly mile-high High Rocks summit. The trail begins a rather long descent. After a switchback, it trav-

els through a moist, rhododendron-laced cove, until the path reaches a sunny junction with Whiteoak Branch Trail. I stop here for a snack. At the junction I spot a rusted shovelhead, which may be a relic from a former farmstead located here.

I begin hiking Whiteoak Branch Trail and soon reach Gray Wolf Creek, which still has enough of a flow to require a short rock-hop across it. I then enter a pleasant open cove, where it's still and silent, except for the rustling of leaves underfoot. After a sharp switchback, the trail descends to a crossing of Whiteoak Branch, before ending at a junction with Forney Creek Trail. The latter path continues straight ahead for travel upstream, and left, across the branch, for hiking downstream. A bear-warning sign is posted on the trail sign where I decide to stop for lunch, keeping food and pack close at hand.

After lunch, there's a stiff, but brief, climb on Forney Creek Trail before a longer descent brings the trail near creek level. For the next 1½ miles of downstream hiking, I enjoy many lovely stream scenes through the rhododendron bordering the trail, including a number of short waterfalls and clear pools. It's relaxing hiking on a gently descending railbed built for logging in pre-park days. The peacefulness is broken only briefly by the short-lived hum of a helicopter, which I'm thinking is on its way to fight a forest fire near the park. I arrive at a junction with Bear Creek Trail and decide to cross Forney Creek on a bridge, which leads to a former backcountry campsite where Karen and I camped on the final night of a four-day backcountry excursion in 1985. I'm not surprised that the site has since been shut down, for it's not particularly inviting, though I have to say it looked pretty good after a grueling hike from Hazel Creek that took us up and over towering Welch Ridge.

Farther downstream, just below the junction of

Forney Creek and Lakeshore Trails, is a more becoming backcountry campsite known as Lower Forney. It's a broad, level site, slightly above the creek, with several suitable tent sites, if not a lot of privacy. The fact that it's a horse site, and a popular one at that, with a hitching post near the middle of the camp, may deter some backpackers from camping here. As I rest on a comfortable log bathed in sunlight, the November sun is almost ready to drop below the trees on the high ridge opposite the creek even though it's only 1:30 P.M.

From here, I turn east onto Lakeshore Trail and begin climbing out of the Forney Creek Valley. As I ascend, I get a glimpse of a finger of Fontana Lake, currently a whopping fifty-five feet below full pool. I also notice that the southwestern sky is changing from blue to a whitish gray, likely from smoke rather than clouds. I cross a bridge over Gray Wolf Creek, below its Whiteoak Branch Trail crossing, and travel an old roadbed for a short distance as I make my way back to the Lakeshore/Whiteoak Branch trail junction. From the junction, it's a steep climb up Forney Ridge, but on the far side of the crest, I'm rewarded with some impressive fall color, enhanced by afternoon sunlight.

Soon after passing a junction with Goldmine Loop Trail, I turn right onto Tunnel Bypass Trail, which takes me back to my car in about 1½ miles. The somewhat narrow path offers views of Welch Ridge and more late-fall color. Less than one half-mile from the car, I reach Goldmine Loop's eastern terminus in an attractive open area. But after a couple of minutes here, I detect a faint smoky smell and notice smoke is in fact building a bit farther down Goldmine Loop Trail. The Smokies are again becoming smokier after a cold front and strong winds had temporarily cleared the air overnight. Fortunately, I completed most of my hike before haze and smoke moved in again and the air became unhealthy to breathe, even for a short period of time. (*Footnote*: On the drive back to Asheville, I saw a forest fire along Interstate 40 West that backed up westbound traffic for many miles.)

In another ten minutes or so, I arrive at the Tunnel Bypass trailhead, where I admire a trail sign that, like one near the road barricade, is made of metal rather than wood. Instead of being painted on, the trail names and distances are perforated into the metal itself. I haven't seen trail signs such as these elsewhere in the Smokies, but they do seem destined to endure at least as long as the North Shore road controversy.

Hike 38

Smoke-free Smokemont

November 20
Trails. Bradley Fork,
    Smokemont Loop
*Trailhead weather
    conditions:* 45 degrees,
    sunny, breezy
Round-trip miles hiked: 6.2

During my most recent visit to Smokemont Campground, in mid-April for a two-night camping trip, a two-hundred-acre wildfire began burning near downtown Cherokee, several miles to the south. I spotted the distant plumes on my way back to camp from a day hike to Charlies Bunion on the Appalachian Trail and later learned that the smoke was indeed from a wildfire in Cherokee. Fortunately, the fire was fully contained within a couple of days—as were two smaller ones elsewhere on the Cherokee Indian Reservation—and no injuries or structural damage resulted, though the largest blaze did force a main road closure for a while.

Threatening as the spring wildfire season was, it barely had an impact compared with the numerous fall wildfires that are now raging across the North Carolina mountains as I return to Smokemont on a day trip. Within the past few weeks, a total of about twenty wildfires have scorched nearly fifty thousand acres in western North Carolina, numbers that unfortunately will continue to grow. Still, the only reported fire in the Smokies as of this date was a short-lived one of about a quarter-acre, which burned at the duff level near the Chimney Tops summit in Tennessee. Nonetheless, that small blaze prompted park officials to close four trails, which I hiked at least parts of this year, for a couple of days. (*Footnote*: Tragically, later in

November in the same area, arsonists started what became a horrific blaze named the Chimney Tops 2 Fire.) The dangerously dry conditions are a dramatic contrast to those at the beginning of the year, right after the Smokies were inundated during a remarkably wet and mild final two months of 2015. Someone has turned off the rainfall spigot this year, and the Smokies are now in the grip of an extreme-to-exceptional drought with no end in sight.

Recently, I stopped at an outdoors shop in Asheville and asked the young woman behind the counter where I could find quadrangles in the spacious store.

"Quadrangles?" she asked, thinking she must not have heard me correctly.

"Yes, you know, the large topographic maps with contour lines," I replied.

"Sorry, we don't carry anything like that," she said.

I realize we're deep into the digital age, but no quadrangles? For an old-school guy like me, that borders on outfitter negligence. Large printed quadrangles—United States Geological Survey topographic maps—remain invaluable in the backcountry in my estimation. Not to mention the fact that they're fun to pore over. But not to worry—another venerable outdoors store on the other side of town still carries drawers and drawers full of them.

The Smokemont Quadrangle, revised in 2000, actually is the most recent topographic map of the Smokies that I have. That's not surprising because the U.S.G.S. began producing "topos" as digital documents in 2009. (*Footnote*: An addition to the 2000 edition that was not on the 1964 version is the place name Mount Stand Watie, a nearly four-thousand-foot mountain that son Rob and I unsuccessfully attempted to reach off-trail on my

first hike of 2016.) But even the quadrangles I have dating to 1964 are still useful. Although trails are rebuilt, rerouted, or abandoned from time to time, natural features and contour lines typically don't change much in a lifetime, barring something like a major earthquake or meteorite strike. Thus, on my hikes I usually carry at least one quadrangle, which can be vital for orientation when used with a compass. In fact, during my travels this year, I have relied upon a total of nearly twenty "quads," most of them courtesy of my late father-in-law, Robert Strippel. And before and after my excursions, I frequently refer to my framed Knoxville relief map on a wall at home, as it encompasses the entire park, and much more, with its horizontal scale of 1:250,000. The map provides an excellent overview of the park's unruly topography, and of the general terrain each hike traverses.

Curiously enough, though, even the most recent printed Smokemont Quadrangle I have does not indicate the longest part of today's hike—Smokemont Loop Trail. This trail courses through rugged territory between two beautiful streams: Bradley Fork and Oconaluftee River. But as with most trails in the Smokies, the route isn't hard to follow. Still, the quadrangle's contour lines at forty-foot intervals show how steep the complete loop is in places as it climbs from about twenty-two hundred feet at the campground to a high point of about thirty-five hundred feet.

On this sunny, cool Sunday before Thanksgiving, Smokemont isn't quite deserted, but undoubtedly it's much quieter than it was a month ago during the height of the fall-color season. The two campground loops that remain open year-round are dotted by just a couple of RVs and pop-up campers and only one tent upon my arrival in early afternoon. And there's no smoke, from the campground or elsewhere, because campfires are currently banned even at the few developed Smokies campgrounds still open this late in the year. My car does join a few other vehicles in the day-use and backcountry parking area, but it seems obvious that I won't encounter many people today on my relatively short hike.

A brisk breeze whips through the closed upper campground loops while I walk toward the trailhead for Bradley Fork Trail, which will lead about 1¾ miles to Smokemont Loop Trail. Yes, it's chilly for November 20 at this elevation, but it's still nothing like this morning's low temperature atop Mount Le Conte: ten degrees, with a wind chill likely below zero. Indian summer may have finally exited the stage. But with plenty of sunshine, afternoon hiking proves to be pleasant, even though the chill lingers on slopes with northern exposure where it's shaded and breezy.

Soon after I start walking on Bradley Fork Trail, which heads upstream along an old roadbed, I see several people—including a couple of youngsters—making their way down a few steps to the stream to fish. A few minutes later, I meet several more people who are walking back toward the campground, curiously carrying sleeping bags not in or attached to backpacks. I'm guessing they managed to make it to Lower Chasteen Creek backcountry campsite, only about 1¼ miles from the trailhead, for a cold overnight. At the junction with Chasteen Creek Trail, someone who may be a trailing member of the same party, is drinking from a gallon jug. The few close-in backcountry campsites in the Smokies seem to attract quite a collection of campers.

At the junction, I turn right onto Chasteen Creek Trail for a short side trip to the Lower Chasteen campsite, where I plan to eat lunch. The main part of the camp is not only mostly protected from the wind, but is also favored by a warming sun on fair winter afternoons. My lunch spot, featuring an upright sawed log that I use for a seat, is nearly spotless, although the same, unfortunately, cannot be said of campsites closer to the creek.

After lunch, I return to Bradley Fork Trail, hiking not far behind a couple walking at a fast pace on this beautiful, blue-sky afternoon. Farther up, at the junction with Smokemont Loop Trail, I see them pausing to study a trail map and ask if I can help. As it turns out the young woman and man are from the Netherlands, visiting the Smokies for several days to enjoy terrain that is vastly different from that of their homeland. They are wondering whether they should turn left on the loop trail and cross Bradley Fork, or continue upstream on the remainder of Bradley Fork Trail. We all agree that the better bet with only a few remaining hours of daylight is Smokemont Loop. Because they're concerned about the rather long and high foot log across Bradley Fork, especially with just a leaning single handrail, the man asks me to cross first so that they can get a better idea of what to expect. Before I proceed, I wish them well, though we will engage in a longer conversation once the trail reaches the crest of Richland Mountain.

Upon crossing Bradley Fork, the trail heads downstream for a short distance before a sharp switchback routes the path uphill on a long, steady ascent, which lacks sun because of northern exposure. During the climb, I see fine views of the lofty Hughes and Mine Ridges to the east. I then top the divide where Richland Mountain begins to make its last stand after descending from fifty-five-hundred-foot Dry Sluice Gap on the Appalachian Trail. At this point, I suddenly enjoy sunshine again, along with the distant sounds of the Oconaluftee River far below and a nice view of Newfound Gap, a few miles northwest. Soon, the trail travels past a copse of pines on the dry ridge, including a couple of quite large ones below the path. After a bit more climbing, the trail attains its apex and begins a long downhill track toward Smokemont Campground.

Near its terminus, the trail reaches a former road-bed, where I decide to turn right in order to visit the Bradley Cemetery, just up the way. (Smokemont was known as Bradleytown before Champion Fibre Company transformed it into a logging and sawmill company town early in the twentieth century.) Most of the over-grown sites are marked by fieldstones, but two actual monuments are especially prominent: those of *Father Jasper Bradley (1851-1924)* and *Mother Palistine Bradley (1859-1922)*. Noted as being *At Rest*, they have similar epitaphs reading, *A tender father and faithful friend* and *A tender mother and faithful friend*. Can progeny ask more of parents than that?

I rejoin the roadbed for the short remaining distance to the campground. The trail ends by crossing an old bridge over Bradley Fork. A sign notes the structure was designed and built by Luten Bridge Company of Knoxville, Tennessee, in 1921—several years before the park was authorized and more than a decade be-fore it was established. The bridge, now gated, thus was commissioned by Swain County, North Carolina, and not by the National Park Service. (*Footnote*: Later in the 1920s, Luten was the losing plaintiff in a lawsuit that is still cited as a landmark case in American contract law.)

As I near the car, I think about my second conversation with the young couple from the Netherlands, once they caught up with me while I rested in a slight gap with a fine view of Thomas Divide. After more trail talk (with their flawless English), I simply could not resist asking them what they thought of our recent presidential election, as I was confident they would be well informed about the United States and its politics. With my question, I put them squarely on the spot in a foreign land, and in a deeply divided state. After some hesitation, the young woman responded exactly as I thought she (and he) would. A few minutes later, as they began to depart after further perceptive comments about the election, she cheerfully added, "But at least you have your Smoky Mountains."

Hike 39

A Dramatic Turn of Events

December 3
Trails: Caldwell Fork,
Boogerman
*Trailhead weather
conditions:* 46 degrees,
mostly cloudy, calm
Round-trip miles hiked: 7.6

As numerous wildfires raged across the southern Appalachians for most of November, the park was spared except for a small fire near Chimney Tops that had a relatively minor impact. Dramatically and tragically, arson in the same area late in the month changed that good fortune. Ironically, it happened just a few days before significant rainfall finally arrived, following three parched months. The park's first major wildfire of the fall fire season, named the Chimney Tops 2 Fire, scorched a sizable portion of the park's forestland in a destructive preview of the nearly twenty-five hundred homes and businesses in and around Gatlinburg that burned during a night of terror November 28-29. (Although some park structures sustained wind damage, somehow the fire itself did not destroy or damage any structures inside the park.) Fed by dry vegetation, low humidity, and winds gusting to hurricane force, the Chimney Tops 2 Fire ultimately grew exponentially from a two-acre blaze on the Chimneys' northern spire. The fast-moving fire raged far beyond a planned four-hundred-acre containment area to become a catastrophic eighteen-thousand-acre inferno inside and outside the park. The fire, which was not fully contained until December 18, forced closure of the entire park for the first time since the needless federal government shutdown in 2013; park headquarters and Newfound Gap

Road did not reopen for ten days. The park-wide shutdown came a day after park officials closed ten backcountry camping areas, about twenty trails, and three roads, including Newfound Gap Road, because of the rapidly growing fire. (*Footnote:* Several of those paths, including the extremely popular Chimney Tops Trail, remained closed well into 2017.) In short, the fire's impact inside and outside the park was historic, devastating, and deadly, as it killed fourteen people and injured or sickened nearly two hundred more. Gatlinburg and Sevier County will never be the same after a truly hellish night.

In the wake of the widespread destruction in the Gatlinburg area, the park's backcountry office understandably asked all volunteers to refrain from any type of volunteer work anywhere in the park until further notice. Because the Chimney Tops 2 Fire was still only 10 percent contained inside the park by early December, backcountry managers obviously wished to keep the focus on firefighters battling the blaze. But with the North Carolina side of the park reopened and unscathed, I decide, after some deliberation, to resume my hiking excursions in a part of the park far removed from fire damage or danger.

From time to time, the isolated Cataloochee Valley has been a kind of refuge for me. It served as such soon after the 9/11 attacks, and today its quiet beauty has a similar effect in the wake of the disastrous Chimney Tops 2 Fire. Perhaps at some point, I can assist in some small way with this latest tragedy, with it occurring close to home. But for now, I find a measure of peace in Cataloochee on this cool December day after a November marked by shocking events. Although I'm usually a warm-weather guy, never having lived north of Greensboro, North Carolina, I do enjoy the quietude and stark beauty of Cataloochee during the winter.

Today I decide to hike the lower section of Caldwell Fork Trail and the entire Boogerman Trail. The latter path is named for one Robert "Boogerman" Palmer, who according to Cataloochee legend told his teacher on the first day of school that his name was Boogerman; not surprisingly, the name endured. Rather than a complete loop, the Caldwell Fork/Boogerman route is shaped more like a lasso as the first three-fourths mile on Caldwell Fork Trail is repeated on the return to the trailhead. Slightly more than half of today's hike is one-way on Boogerman Trail.

Today the tight, twisting road into Cataloochee seems rougher, more rutted, than it did on my October trip to the valley. But it's also considerably less dusty, because of the long-anticipated rainfall earlier in the week. Traffic is also much lighter, as one would expect in December, even on a Saturday. The long-range views are good, too, with the deciduous trees now essentially bare. I make it to the park boundary in less than an hour from my house and to trailhead parking in another fifteen minutes or so. I'm surprised to see three vehicles at the small parking area upon my arrival, though there's still adequate space for mine.

Caldwell Fork Trail begins with the most attractive footbridge I've seen, a structure that spans Palmer Creek. Recently and beautifully constructed with stone steps and footings and a long planed log, it also features double wooden handrails that make the wide creek crossing safer and less intimidating. The footbridge provides a sharp contrast to some of the trail's aging foot logs, and especially to Caldwell Fork crossings that require fording of the stream where former foot logs have washed out.

The first part of Caldwell Fork Trail is easy and pleasant. On mostly level terrain, it courses through a mixed open forest, featuring many tall white pines. After about one-third mile, the trail bends to the left to run along the west side of Caldwell Fork, before crossing the stream on another sturdy, reconstructed footbridge. It then reaches an unassuming junction with Boogerman Trail, where I turn left and rock-hop across Palmer Branch (not to be confused with Palmer Creek). Here the trail begins a steady climb in the general direction of soaring Cataloochee Divide, eventually attaining an elevation above thirty-five hundred feet at its highest point. Initially the tread on the trail—the only one in Cataloochee that's off-limits to horse traffic—is easy on the feet, punctuated by soft pine needles underfoot in many places. About halfway along the four-mile trail, the path passes the site of the former home and farm of Boogerman Palmer. I pull in for lunch after a stiff, mostly straight, climb to a wintertime view spot along Den Ridge.

The high clouds continue to thicken, while I eat a ham-and-cheese sandwich instead of my usual peanut butter and jelly. It's become a dark December afternoon, with the temperature stubbornly hanging in the mid-forties. I'm beginning to wonder if the rain predicted to move in overnight might arrive this afternoon. Suddenly, I feel enveloped by what my conservation hero Theodore Roosevelt called the melancholy of the wilderness. But the loneliness of this spot will soon yield to signs of civilization, which come from seeing the vestiges of past homesteads and encountering other hikers. I have another sip of water and start hiking again.

Soon, I begin a cardio climb to the trail's apex, where there's a view through the leafless trees of mighty Mount Sterling. A milky sun reappears, brightening the winter woods. I start to descend on a trail that will be rougher and rockier for most of its remaining course to its upper junction with Caldwell Fork Trail. After the grade eases at an old homesite to the right of the trail, there's a long, low rock wall, which has stood the test of time despite its absence of mortar. Just down the trail is a large, hollowed-out yellow poplar, so much a prototype for a bear den that it may as well have a welcome mat out front. The trail then begins to play tag with Snake Branch, crossing it in a few places, before passing another rock wall. I get a glimpse of hikers down the trail before I see another rock wall. Here a short side trail leads steeply to a ridge, where twisted barbed-wire fencing encloses two graves marked by fieldstones. Before reaching Caldwell Fork Trail, I catch up with three hikers. As they clear limb debris, one says that they're doing some impromptu trail maintenance. I reply by noting that's never a bad thing. After turning right on Caldwell Fork Trail, back toward the trailhead, I traverse one last short crossing of Snake Branch before the latter finally disappears into the fork.

For the next couple of miles, until Caldwell Fork Trail meets the lower Boogerman Trail, the stream crosses the trail numerous times. Unfortunately for hikers, several crossings require fords that are not only bone-chilling to feet and legs in the winter, but also are a little treacherous in places, even with low water. A misstep and fall into the cold December water could quickly lead to hypothermia. Even some of the foot logs still in place are missing handrails. At the first ford, I dig out creek shoes from my daypack. Despite their uncomfortable wetness, I doggedly keep them on—even as I travel on land—for other creeks I'll need to ford before I gladly reach the Boogerman junction. Just beyond the junction, I put my dry hiking shoes and socks back on, grateful that two sturdy footbridges will keep me dry the rest of the way, unless I do something really crazy. I don't, and find myself back at the car after about fifteen more minutes of dry, enjoyable walking.

At trail's end, I decide to drive farther up the valley, to where it opens up into lovely meadows framed by soaring mountains. En route, near a ranger residence, the last of a dozen or so wild turkeys are crossing the road. But their numbers are surpassed by an even larger group of elk cows that have gathered between the road and house. It's a pastoral and peaceful landscape, almost poignantly so, considering the events on the Tennessee side of the Smokies earlier this week. Sadly, the Gatlinburg area is facing a long and difficult road back from the cataclysmic Chimney Tops 2 Fire, and even that is understatement.

Hike 40

Of Hogs and Horace

December 13
Trail: Noland Creek
*Trailhead weather
  conditions:* 38 degrees,
  overcast, calm
Round-trip miles hiked: 13.0

For a route that has long been derisively called The Road to Nowhere, Lake View Drive certainly leads to an inviting part of the park. But yes, it does end a long way from its originally intended destination near Fontana Dam. Today, on my final planned trip in the Smokies for this year, I travel the road again in order to hike out and back on more than half of the ten-mile Noland Creek Trail. Although the lower part of Noland Creek often flows at a relatively languid pace for a stream in the Smokies, on this mid-December day it's running fairly fast, thanks to recent rainfall that has provided some long-awaited relief to the drought-stricken park. Even so, this section of the creek seems in no great hurry to join Fontana Lake to the south.

It's clammy and gloomy upon my arrival at a large parking area, located just before the long, curving bridge high above Noland Creek. There's no car in sight except for a park-service vehicle that cruises by. Although dry for now, rain—a cold rain—is likely on the way. I ask myself if I really want to set out on what I hope will be a twelve- or thirteen-mile hike round-trip. The answer is yes, as I've committed to it with a one-hundred-minute drive from my house. After opting for heavier hiking boots, I walk down the steep, rocky access trail to Noland Creek Trail, well below the parking lot. At the latter path, I turn right, hiking away from the path's Fontana Lake terminus and toward a junction with Noland Divide Trail. The junction is nine miles away, so I won't reach it today. The tri-state Benton MacKaye Trail piggybacks the nine-mile section as it works its way northeast between Forney Ridge and Noland Divide, a stretch that climbs mostly gradually from less than two thousand to more than four thousand feet at the divide. But today, I plan to make it to an elevation of only about three thousand feet before turning back.

After walking beneath the soaring bridge span and crossing Noland Creek on a wooden bridge, I begin an easy ascent on the trail, which follows an old roadbed. The gray December forest, with its absence of foliage, provides a stark contrast to my last trip here on a sunny September afternoon, when the vegetation was almost jungle-like. But today rhododendron and doghobble are all that impede—and just slightly—view after view of a lovely Smokies stream.

Within a half hour, I reach a short side trail that leads to some mid-1980s memories, courtesy of Bear Pen Branch backcountry campsite. Situated where a school once stood, the campsite was then the jumping-off point for a couple of two-night backpacking trips. I rock-hop across the small branch to reach the site, a backcountry rarity in that it has picnic tables. Tall hemlock trees stand guard over the narrow, sloping camp. Leaning against one tree is a shock-corded tent pole that campers abandoned or forgot—likely the latter as it is still in good condition. As I rest at one of the tables, a few sprinkles start to fall, prompting me to don a rain jacket before I walk back to the main trail.

After returning to Noland Creek Trail, I climb the path, rising above a retaining wall, where I proceed to walk briskly on the gently graded roadbed. In about one half-mile, the trail passes through a handsome grove of towering white pines. Soon, the sprinkles become a light rain, and I begin to ponder how wet I am willing to get in forty-degree weather. I make a decision: if the rain seems heavy enough to halt a baseball game when I reach a junction with Springhouse Branch Trail about 4¼ miles from my starting point, I plan to turn back. In the meantime, a series of creek crossings won't be an issue, as they will be accomplished via wide—if slippery in places—wooden bridges. Soon, I reach Solola Valley, a formerly populated area, where a log flume operated in the early twentieth century. (Commercial logging on Noland Creek actually began in the late 1880s.) In a few more minutes, I arrive at the trail junction, site of the expansive Mill Creek backcountry camp. By now the rain has stopped altogether, so I decide to poke around the site that not only has picnic tables of its own, but also a long hitching post with a battered horse trough.

About two hundred yards above the Mill Creek camp, just past a rock overhang, Noland Creek Trail traverses the stream on a rustically elegant footbridge, which features double handrails in the form of slender logs, similar to the bridge crossing Palmer Creek at the Caldwell Fork trailhead. Straight across the creek is the foundation wall of a former home. Within another mile, after the roadbed has yielded to a narrower, rockier trail, there's a less elaborate foot log, positioned several feet above what has become, with the elevation change, a pushier Noland Creek. I hike past the Jerry Flats backcountry camp, where a side trail to the left leads to a cemetery, and then cross Noland Creek on yet another foot log. After a slight dip, the trail arrives at a wide creek crossing that is the end of the line for me, because the trail requires fording in the absence of a footbridge. With the temperature struggling to top forty degrees, I'm not inclined to go wading in nearly knee-deep water six-plus miles from the trailhead. I reverse course in order to return to Jerry Flats, where a sign notes that the campsite is closed because of aggressive bear activity. I decide not to eat lunch in the middle of the camp, choosing instead a nearby off-trail spot. Soon, I'll see a different type of large animal—an ill-mannered sort not welcome in the park.

There is a wild hog in these woods
Doodle um-day
There is a wild hog in these woods
Doodle um oh day
There is a wild hog in these woods that
eats men's flesh and drinks their blood
Cut him down
Cut him down
Catch him if you can

– from an old ballad

Yes, there's a wild hog in these woods—actually hundreds of them, or more. They are the descendants of about fifteen European wild boar that were brought to a private game preserve on Hooper Bald, southwest of the Smokies, in the early twentieth century. Local residents began referring to the boar as "black Russians" or "Rooshians," thinking they came from the Ural Mountains of Russia; more likely, they were from Germany or Poland. At any rate, their numbers multiplied rapidly before about one hundred escaped the fenced preserve and disappeared into the surrounding area. They arrived in the southwestern corner of the park around mid-century and proceeded to establish themselves as easily the park's largest exotic species. Some boars exceed three hundred pounds. Although the boar is often nocturnal and rarely seen, signs of its rooting and wal-

lowing are not uncommon, as the Rooshians essentially become hairy bulldozers in their unrelenting search for just about any kind of food. The boar—prosaically called wild or feral hogs by the park service because of breeding with domestic hogs—is cunning, stealthy, and ornery. The critter also is likely here to stay, despite being slowed by the viral disease *pseudorabies* and ongoing park efforts to control the population by trapping and hunting. In fact, the park service has removed more than twelve thousand boars from the Smokies since 1959—eight thousand times more than the fifteen or so that came here originally.

I note all this because this afternoon I'm startled to see my first wild boar of the year. After dozens of outings and more than 420 miles of hiking, the sighting occurs just a few miles from the end of my travels. He's about fifty yards down trail before dashing away in an impressive imitation of Olympics champion Usain Bolt. (Boars actually can run as fast as thirty miles per hour—faster than Bolt's fastest short distance.) He stops, and then takes off again when he sees I'm still headed his way. When I round the next bend, he charges off a third time before finally taking a right turn off-trail into the woods. He waits there watchfully until I pass, and then heads back at a slower pace toward his original spot that I have apparently intruded upon. Perhaps the Rooshian has finally finished his afternoon wind sprints.

After the entertaining boar show, I resume hiking at a fast pace, partly because drizzle has returned. As the trail rises well above the creek in some places and runs alongside it in others, I continue to enjoy the creek's many beautiful stream scenes, featuring crystal-clear water. I briefly consider continuing on Noland Creek Trail to its southern terminus at a finger of Fontana Lake, thereby adding two miles round-trip to today's excursion. Alas, a light rain starts to fall again by the time I reach the access trail to the parking area, and, no, Fontana Lake is not in the cards today, even with my rain gear. Instead, I reluctantly hike up the short path that connects to the parking lot, wistful that my year of hiking in the Smokies is ending. The cold rain suits my subdued mood.

Some of us outlanders who are attracted to live in or near the Great Smoky Mountains consider Bryson City a sort of spiritual home. Yes, it's a lovely little town on the edge of the park, but it's also where Horace Kephart, Smokies champion and *Our Southern Highlanders* author, lived during the final two decades of his life. More than a century after its initial publication, the influential work and Kephart himself continue to be debated, stirring strong feelings among detractors and admirers alike. (Despite Kephart's personal failings, I'm firmly in the latter category.) One Appalachian historian, for example, wrote that Kephart "completely distorted and misrepresented mountain life and customs," adding that he depicted mountain people as "wretched backward creatures living in depravity and degradation." That would not be my reading of *Our Southern Highlanders*. In my view the book was written by a perceptive observer, one who lived among the people he wrote about, describing what he called their picturesque ways and charm of originality. And apparently, many of them held the sometimes inscrutable "Kep" and his work in very high regard.

Soon after finishing today's hike—my fortieth excursion of the year into the Smokies—I find myself on School House Hill, overlooking holiday-bedecked Bryson City and the much higher terrain rising in the distance. As the season provides some cheer on what is now a dark, rainy December afternoon, I'm here to revisit Kephart's gravesite. It's marked by a massive boulder in a prominent location in Bryson City Cemetery, which is lovingly cared for by a friends group. Yes, I'm unapologetically paying homage to Horace after my year of hiking. It seems only fitting to do so, for Kephart wrote and worked tirelessly to promote the creation of Great Smoky Mountains National Park. For example, in a magazine article published in 1926—the year the park was authorized—he wrote that if the Smokies' remaining primeval forests could be saved "it will be a joy and a wonder to our people for all time." In the light rain, I reflect for a few minutes on Kephart's accomplishments and unconventional journey in life, as well as on my humble hiking year that began nearly fifty weeks ago on New Year's Day. On this latest of many visits to his resting place, I am moved, as always, by the unembellished words on the boulder's plaque:

HORACE KEPHART
1862-1931

SCHOLAR, AUTHOR, OUTDOORSMAN.
HE LOVED HIS NEIGHBORS
AND PICTURED THEM IN

"OUR SOUTHERN HIGHLANDERS"

HIS VISION HELPED TO CREATE
THE GREAT SMOKY MOUNTAINS
NATIONAL PARK

Tragically, Kephart died in an automobile accident three years before the park was established; his esteem was such that people packed the local high school auditorium for his funeral. But as Kephart scholar George Ellison noted, he departed this life knowing that the park would become a reality. Thus, his beloved forests would be spared further desecration by large-scale logging operations. Kephart's determined efforts, along with those of many others, gave succeeding generations a gift that should not be taken for granted. As for me personally, the gift I've received from Kephart and his fellow park advocates and benefactors is immeasurable: more than thirty years of adventures in the Smokies, none more memorable than an eventful year of hiking at age sixty-four.

Epilogue

It's December 31—my sixty-fifth birthday—and I've decided to end the year the way I started it: with a short hike up Mingus Creek. The full-circle thing, one might say. Only this time out, son Ben and his wife, Ashley, join son Rob and me on our trek. Before starting on Mingus Creek Trail, we walk up a faint path from the parking area in order to visit the site of several graves of enslaved people. Their final resting places are humbly marked by small fieldstones. Once we join Mingus Creek Trail, Rob and I observe that although the weather is almost identical to that of the first day of 2016, the path itself isn't nearly as wet. From the junction about 1¼ mile out, we retrace the route to Mingus Cemetery, less than a mile up a side trail. On the way back on the main trail, we see several hikers, plus a couple of dogs off-leash. I remind their owners that, as the sign at the trailhead notes, dogs aren't allowed in the backcountry—leashed or unleashed. I don't press the issue when they continue on anyway. (So much for my authority.) Before we reach the parking lot, I see the first few snowflakes I've seen this year while hiking in the Smokies. We will see many more driving back on the Blue Ridge Parkway from Oconaluftee to Soco Gap, before exiting onto U.S. Highway 19 toward Asheville.

What specifically did I learn on my travels in the Smokies during 2016? Certainly too much to recount in a nice, neat summary. But very broadly, I learned that published trail guides and maps about the Smokies are generally reliable, if sometimes outdated rather quickly. Trails are rebuilt, rerouted, even closed. Thus, hikers should never rely completely on trail descriptions—even aside from the fact that tree blowdowns, swollen streams, and the like can create sudden and unexpected challenges. Nevertheless, traveling on established and maintained trails is typically far easier—not to mention safer—than venturing off-trail, especially when hiking alone. Most of the off-trail terrain is too unruly, and the undergrowth too dense, to navigate without extreme effort and expertise.

Perhaps some would differ, but I also found that most of the official park trails I hiked were generally well maintained, thanks to the maintenance and rehabilitation efforts of park-service employees and volunteers. For example, extensive work to rehabilitate upper Forney Ridge Trail transformed a wet, rocky, somewhat treacherous path into one that is now much easier and more enjoyable to hike for the thousands who travel it each year to reach alluring Andrews Bald. Although fire forced their closure for varying periods late in 2016, the heavily traveled Alum Cave and Chimney Tops Trails also benefited from recent restorations. Not surprisingly, often the trails in relatively poor condition are those on which horses are allowed. But heavy foot traffic and unusually wet routes can exact a stiff toll too, as evident on parts of the Appalachian Trail and other extremely popular paths. And the fact that several footbridges have been out for years on Caldwell Fork Trail—along with foot logs on other paths such as Fork Ridge Trail where it and North Carolina's Mountains-to-Sea Trail cross Deep Creek—can't be blamed on extensive horse use.

Among the year's many memorable sights—too many to list—were rushing waterfalls, lovely wildflowers, vivid fall color, and stunning vistas along and near the great crest of the Smokies, along with a couple of black bears at close range and a wild boar that seemed to play something of a cat-and-mouse game with me. But none was more memorable than the long-range views on the rarest of June days atop storied Mount Le Conte. Little wonder that so many people have hiked so many times to its summit, on both day and overnight visits. And no sights were more jaw-dropping than the long-range panoramas from atop Shuckstack fire tower on a magnificent August afternoon, and from Rocky Top on an equally gorgeous September day. As for the Smokies' rugged terrain in general, yes, there are many higher mountain ranges on earth, as well as perhaps more striking ones, if one favors rocky, jagged, or snow-covered peaks. I'm not sure if any mountains are more captivating, especially across four seasons that are as distinct as they are lengthy. But as an adopted son of the Smokies, I admit to some bias.

Much as I appreciated the Great Smokies before the year began, my regard for the park was greater still by year's end. On my outings, I continually found the Smokies to be as scenic and diverse as other eastern parks such as Acadia, Congaree, and Everglades are distinctive. In my view, our most heavily visited national park easily qualifies as a national treasure, one that demands sound stewardship on multiple fronts, especially given the Smokies' ongoing ecological threats, visitor impacts, and insufficient funding. (If "America's Best Idea" is our national parks, our worst one is not funding them adequately.) Even if GSMNP isn't a park in peril—as some national parks may be from climate change and other factors—it clearly is one that continues to face significant challenges from both inside and outside its boundary lines. For example, although air quality within the park has improved significantly since the late 1990s—thanks in large part to the installation of sulfur-dioxide scrubbers on nearby TVA coal-fired power plants—park rainfall remains five times more acidic than natural rainfall because of sulfur and nitrogen pollution.

I often wonder what the Great Smoky Mountains would look like today if they hadn't become a national park in the mid-1930s. Certainly there would be fewer pockets of old-growth forest if the park's creation hadn't halted the voracious logging industry in its tracks. And although much of the Smokies' rumpled topography seems inhospitable to development, it's likely that even much of the higher terrain would be heavily developed with gated-community homes, jarring tourist attractions, garish billboards, and assorted other commercial endeavors. (Tourism-related development in communities near the park proceeded rapidly and essentially unimpeded soon after World War II. Regrettably, much of that development—successful or not—has been in harsh contrast to the natural beauty of the park.) Not that the National Park Service has left the Smokies completely undisturbed, of course. In our national parks, there is likely to always be tension between preserving their natural state and providing services and infrastructure so that the public can enjoy the parks. But roads and structures built in the Smokies park after its creation have generally reflected sensitivity to the stunning landscape. Certainly there have been missteps as park managers wrestled with the extent and role of human impact—past and present—in the Smokies, but fortunately several ill-conceived park road projects that would have devoured a great deal more forestland were ultimately scrapped. As it is, the park has no shortage of roads: a total of nearly four hundred miles, most of them paved, penetrating the forests. Yet, on balance, I think the park service has heeded the famous admonition of Theodore Roosevelt, our pioneering conservation president, and applied it beyond the Grand Canyon he was referring to specifically with these remarks: "Leave it as it is. You cannot improve on it. The ages have been at work on it, and man can only mar it."

Perhaps I should note in closing this chronicle that I don't regard my 400-plus miles (actually 430, including the short Mingus Creek reprise, on 71 different trails) of Smokies hiking during 2016 as some sort of remarkable achievement, nor did I ever intend it to be viewed as such. I might have come close to hiking all eight hundred miles of trails in the park had I recruited other drivers for drop-offs and car switches, and planned considerably more outings and car travel on my part. But even if I had walked every inch of every trail in the Smokies, I would still fall short of being familiar with the entire 520,000-acre park. No one, I would submit, can know all of it from hiking all its paths—such is the mystery of the wilderness and vastness of the park beyond its trails and roads. In any case, 2016 proved to be an unforgettable year of exploring and hiking in our most heavily visited national park as the National Park Service turned one hundred years old.

Favorite Hikes by Month

Primary or Sole Trail Noted First, Followed by Destination if Different

January—Maddron Bald/Albright Grove

February—Ramsey Cascades

March—Noland Divide/Lonesome Pine

April—Kephart Prong/Charlies Bunion

May—Snake Den Ridge/Cosby Knob

June—The Boulevard/Mount Le Conte

July—Cataloochee Divide/Purchase Knob

August—Appalachian/Shuckstack

September—Lead Cove/Thunderhead

October—Chestnut Branch/Mount Cammerer

November—Lakeshore/Forney Creek

December—Noland Creek

Favorite Lookouts

Alphabetical by Place Name, Followed by Trail Name if Different

Andrews Bald/Forney Ridge (Hike 19)

Brushy Mountain (Hike 36)

Charlies Bunion/Appalachian (Hike 13)

Clingmans Dome Observation Tower/Appalachian (Hike 19)

Gregory Bald (Hike 20)

Heintooga Overlook/Flat Creek (Hike 22)

Lonesome Pine/Noland Divide (Hike 10)

Mount Cammerer Fire Tower/Mount Cammerer (Hike 31)

Mount Sterling Fire Tower/Baxter Creek (Hike 28)

Myrtle Point/The Boulevard (Hike 18)

Rocky Top/Appalachian (Hike 30)

Shuckstack Fire Tower/Appalachian (Hike 26)

Index